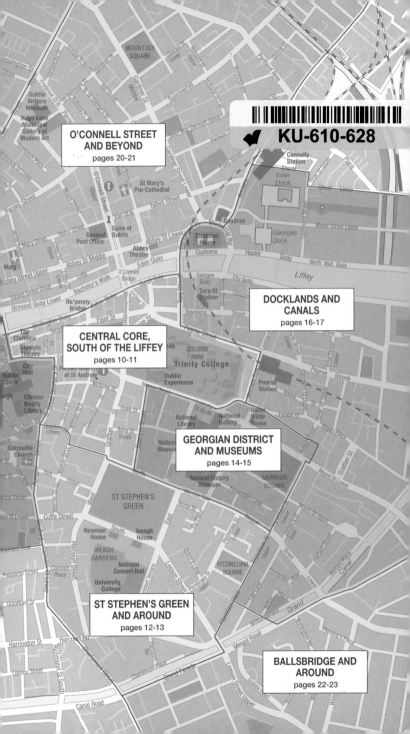

KU-610-628

O'CONNELL STREET AND BEYOND
pages 20-21

DOCKLANDS AND CANALS
pages 16-17

CENTRAL CORE, SOUTH OF THE LIFFEY
pages 10-11

GEORGIAN DISTRICT AND MUSEUMS
pages 14-15

ST STEPHEN'S GREEN AND AROUND
pages 12-13

BALLSBRIDGE AND AROUND
pages 22-23

INSIGHT GUIDES

DUBLIN

smart guide

Contents

Highlights

▲ **Temple Bar** The heart of Dublin's nightlife scene.

▼ **Kilmainham Gaol** Tour the cells of this famous institution to reveal Dublin's turbulent past and the lives of the men and women who fought for freedom.

▲ **Trinity College and the Book of Kells** Walk around the illustrious campus and catch a glimpse of the famous Irish manuscript.

▲ **National Museum and National Gallery** These magnificent institutions house some of Ireland's greatest treasures.

▲ **Traditional pubs and the craic** Irish pubs are legendary the world over for their craic, and Dublin offers ample chance to enjoy this unique tradition.

◄ **Guinness Storehouse** Celebrating Dublin's most famous brew and the history behind it.

Dublin

Dublin has seen phenomenal growth since the 1990s, witnessing a huge programme of redevelopment and a surge in the economy. The Celtic Tiger's roar may be a bit muted as a result of world recession, but Dubliners are a naturally optimistic bunch, and this vibrant cosmopolitan city, with its fascinating history, individual ways and outgoing people, is still very enjoyable to visit.

Dublin Facts and Figures

Population: 506,000 (city);
1,187,000 (metropolitan area)
Area: 115 sq km (44 sq miles)
Gaelic name: Baile Átha Cliath
Religion: 91% of the population is Catholic
Pubs: around 1,000
Average January temperature: 5°C (41°F)
Average July temperature: 17°C (63°F)
Annual rainfall: 73cm (28.7in)
Biggest park: Phoenix Park is the largest urban park in Europe
Unique bridge: O'Connell Bridge is the only bridge in Europe that is as wide as it is long

History and Geography

There can be few places in the Western world with a more turbulent history and struggle for freedom than Ireland, and Dublin has played a pivotal role in that history. That the light-hearted spirit and friendliness of Dubliners has survived through war, famine and conflict is a tribute to that unique Irishness that is still retained today.

Ireland is naturally a wet country, with nothing between it and the coast of Newfoundland in Canada. Prevailing winds bring low-pressure weather systems in from the Atlantic and, although Dublin fares slightly better by being on the more protected east coast, you should always be prepared for rain, and then when the sun shines it's a bonus.

Cosmopolitan City

While Dubliners retain their Irish identity, the city is becoming increasingly cosmopolitan, with a varied ethnic mix. The largest minority group is Chinese, but there are more and more people arriving from Eastern Europe, in particular Poland and Lithuania.

In 2008 Dublin was said to be the fifth-richest city in the world but also one of the most expensive in Europe. Dublin now not only has a pub culture but a café culture, with an influx of international restaurants. In Temple Bar alone you can experience a traditional Irish meal, authentic Mexican, an Italian pasta dish and even a Nepalese meze. Trendy office workers and visitors from across the globe rub shoulders in the new gastropubs and wine bars that have sprung up all over the city.

New Dublin

Nothing can overshadow the impact of superb Georgian buildings such as Trinity College and Custom House, and the appeal of the city's first-class museums and galleries, the proud legacy of the Victorian age, continues apace. There are, however, some new kids on the block, bringing a new dimension to the skyline of the city. The Docklands and Grand Canal developments are well under way, introducing a different image with gleaming modern office blocks,

Below: Trinity College is a popular attraction as well as a prestigious place to study.

Above: an aerial view of Dublin reveals the city's sprawl out to the sea.

cultural venues, residential apartments and shopping malls. The once depressed and run-down areas are now shiny new beacons of innovation, all with the latest 'green' credentials. Dublin looks set to offer future visitors a perfect blend of old and new, of tradition and modernism, and after several centuries of turning its back on the River Liffey, the waterways are once again at the heart of the city.

Location, Location, Location

Choosing a place to stay is part of the excitement of a trip to Dublin. The various localities can deliver a totally different outlook on the city. If you like to party and be right in the thick of things, the natural choice is Temple Bar. But beware, in some hotel rooms you could be kept awake by the noise into the early hours. The Georgian district, around St Stephen's Green and Merrion Square, offers a more genteel atmosphere, with some delectable townhouses and elegant hotels that offer luxury and sophistication, within a few feet of the city's main attractions and excellent shopping. If you prefer more peaceful, greener surroundings, try desirable Ballsbridge in the southern suburbs, just a short bus ride from the action. An increasing number of visitors prefer to stay in the ultra-modern Docklands district, with popular gastropubs, chic cocktail bars and trendy restaurants right on the doorstep. Although most of the major sights, attractions and entertainment are located within the city-centre core, public transport is excellent, making most places you want to visit within easy reach. Beyond the city environs there's another world, and the DART (Dublin Area Rapid Transit) light-rail system provides the opportunity to explore the coastal settlements and beautiful countryside.

Dubliners

One thing that hasn't changed about Dublin is the cheeky charm of its inhabitants. The Irish have a unique way of welcoming you to their proud city – as if they are inviting you into their home for a pint. Their sense of humour and wit are second to none, and it's true what they say, there's a twinkle in their eye. Besides all the obvious attractions that Dublin can offer, it's that special Irishness and the chance to join in the craic and not to take the world too seriously that makes a visit so memorable.

Far West and Phoenix Park

L ying to the west of the tightly packed city core, the combination of open space, new residential buildings, national museums and the run-down area around the Guinness brewery sheds a different light on the city. One major attraction is the vast Phoenix Park, a great green lung for Dubliners to flock to on a sunny summer's day and an ideal place to take children. The area has its dark side, too, and a tour round Kilmainham Gaol will reveal something of Dublin's turbulent past.

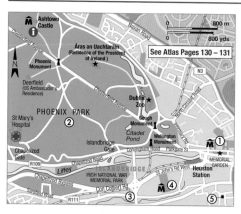

See Atlas Pages 130 – 131

COLLINS BARRACKS

These barracks housed Irish army garrisons and British armed forces through three centuries before being decommissioned and converted to the **National Museum of**

Ireland, Decorative Arts and History ①. Opposite the barracks and facing the river at Croppy's Acre is a **memorial garden** marking the spot where many of those executed, following the 1798 rebellion, are buried.
SEE ALSO MUSEUMS AND GALLERIES, P.80

WESTERN PARKS

To get out of the busy city, especially if you have children, take a trip to **Phoenix Park** ②, the largest enclosed public city park in Europe at 700

Left: a cold winter's day in Phoenix Park.

hectares (1,730 acres) and encircled by a 13km (8-mile) wall. Phoenix Park was originally a royal hunting ground and opened to the public in 1747. Political meetings are integral to the history of the park, the first being held in 1792. Drunkenness, gambling and hurling matches on Sundays were reported through the centuries, interspersed with Temperance rallies to rid the city of the demon drink.

Entering by the Parkgate Street entrance you will soon encounter the huge **Wellington Monument** (1747), a 62m (205ft) granite obelisk. Further monuments scattered throughout the park include the Phoenix Monument and the striking 28m (92ft) stainless steel Papal Cross.

Within the confines of the park is **Dublin Zoo**, founded in 1882 and the second-oldest in Europe. The oldest building in Phoenix Park is 15th-century **Ashtown Castle**, which is located beside the Visitor Centre. Important state buildings include **Áras an Uachtaráin**, the official residence of the President of Ireland; Deerfield, the US

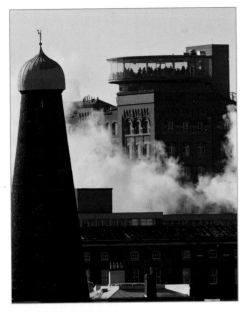

of Modern Art ④. Located in the former Royal Hospital, an initially problematic building for displaying art, it has now been converted into a first-class venue for viewing international and Irish modern art.
SEE ALSO MUSEUMS AND GALLERIES, P.78, 79

THE GUINNESS PHENOMENON

The most popular attraction in Dublin, the **Guinness Storehouse** ⑤ is located at St James's Gate, one of the less attractive, more run-down areas of the city but an important part of the Guinness family empire. The production of Guinness and the family's fortunes have been central to the development of Dublin since 1759, and the brewery has played a major part in employment – 2009 marked 250 years of Guinness production.
SEE ALSO MUSEUMS AND GALLERIES, P.78

Above: at the excellent Irish Museum of Modern Art.

Ambassador's home; and Farmleigh, the State Guest House, which adjoins the park to the northwest.

Well off the tourist track, the **Irish National War Memorial Park** is located on the south bank of the River Liffey opposite Phoenix Park. Designed by architect Edward Lutyens, the attractive gardens are dedicated to the 49,000 Irish soldiers who died in World War I, and their names are etched in two granite book rooms.
SEE ALSO PARKS AND GARDENS, P.96

KILMAINHAM DISTRICT

This district is home to two remarkable attractions. The first is the notorious **Kilmainham Gaol** ③, a forbidding prison on the Inchicore Road and a symbol of political martyrdom and oppression. Here is a chilling reminder of the consequences of the struggle for independence and the lengths the passionate rebels would go to. Originally a prison for common criminals, its role in the political fate of a nation culminated in its use to incarcerate and execute the perpetrators of the Easter Rising of 1916.

To the east of the gaol, in complete contrast, is the exemplary **Irish Museum**

The Phoenix Park Murders of 1882 not only struck terror among politicians but among society in general. Lord Frederick Cavendish, the British Secretary for Ireland and his undersecretary Thomas Henry Burke were stabbed to death by a Fenian splinter group, the 'Irish National Invincibles'. Cavendish, the nephew of British Prime Minister Gladstone, had only arrived in Ireland the day he was murdered. On turning evidence against one another, three of the group were sentenced to penal servitude and five were hanged.

South of the Liffey, West

Moving east from Kilmainham towards two great Protestant cathedrals is the area known as the Liberties. This district has witnessed turbulent times and dire poverty, and in recent years has been the subject of planned redevelopment, provoking huge opposition from residents wishing to retain one of the oldest surviving parts of the city. Early history is recreated at Dublinia and the Viking World museum and witnessed in the oldest churches in the city. The role of state and government is represented at Dublin Castle and the City Hall. Round off with some interesting museums and you will find this area is well worth a visit.

VIKING AND MEDIEVAL DUBLIN

There was an early Christian settlement established in the 5th century around the **Liberties**. The Vikings attacked, plundered and marauded during the 9th and 10th centuries, establishing a trading station in Dublin in AD841 near Kilmainham, and moving downstream to the area around Dublin Castle in the 10th century. Brian Boru defeated the Vikings in 1014 and Irish kings ruled until the arrival of the Normans in 1172.

The earliest surviving buildings of this period are **Christ Church Cathedral** ① commissioned in 1172, and **St Audeon's**, dating from around 1190. The **Brazen Head pub** in Bridge Street occupies the site of possibly the

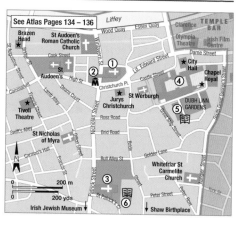

See Atlas Pages 134 – 136

oldest pub in Ireland, dating from 1198. To learn more of these periods of history and the impact they had on the modern city, you can visit **Dublinia and the Viking World** ②, which gives a fascinating insight into the early city through interactive exhibits and a full-scale model of early Dublin.

Following on from Christ Church, **St Patrick's Cathedral** ③ lying to the south was completed in 1192 and is the largest church in Ireland. It was elevated to cathedral status in 1219. Despite most citizens remaining Roman

Catholics, both St Patrick's and Christ Church came under the auspices of the Anglican Church of Ireland after the Reformation in the 16th century, and remain so to this day.
SEE ALSO CHURCHES, P.42; MUSEUMS AND GALLERIES, P.81

CIVIC DUBLIN

Beyond Christ Church, as you head towards the city centre, **Dublin Castle** ④ looms large to your right. Most of the present complex dates from the 18th century, although there has been a castle on the site since the 12th century. Once the headquar-

---

St Patrick's Park provides a welcome refuge for office workers to eat their lunch and for tourists to recharge their batteries after touring the cathedrals or visiting the museums. It is here that Cromwell's troops once planted cabbages, thus introducing the vegetable to Ireland.

Left: Dublin Castle.

Archbishop Narcissus Marsh, scholar, philosopher and scientist, founded Marsh's Library in 1701. He translated the Old Testament into Irish and was an expert on caterpillars and insects, as well as being fascinated by scientific instruments. His Christian name, Narcissus, may have been unusual, but spare a thought for his brothers, who were named Epaphroditus and Onesiphorus. He is buried in the grounds of St Patrick's Cathedral.

ters of English rule, its role today is primarily as a venue for state occasions and civic functions. Within its walls are some interesting and varied museums to visit, and the State Apartments, which can be viewed on a tour along with the **Powder Tower**. The crypt of the **Chapel Royal** is used as an arts centre.

Next door to the castle is **Dublin City Hall**, a fine Georgian edifice built in the 1770s. It was originally the Royal Exchange, assuming its civic role in the 1850s. Most of the council staff has been relocated to the Dublin Civic Offices on the site of the Viking city foundations on Wood Quay. The City Hall is used for council meetings and acts as a function centre.
SEE ALSO MUSEUMS AND
GALLERIES, P.81

ART, BOOKS AND MUSEUMS

Housed in the former revenue offices of Dublin Castle is one of the treasures of Dublin, the **Chester Beatty Library** ⑤. Its title would suggest it was a collection of books and manuscripts, but in addition it has a superb array of oriental art and artefacts. Another excellent

collection of scholarly tomes can be viewed at **Marsh's Library** ⑥, in the close adjacent to St Patrick's Cathedral.

To the south of the area are two small but fascinating museums. The **Irish Jewish Museum**, housed in an old synagogue, lies in the Portbello district, once home to a thriving Jewish community. Meanwhile, the **Shaw Birthplace** is a must for any George Bernard Shaw aficionado or for those interested in the living conditions of the late 19th century.
SEE ALSO MUSEUMS AND
GALLERIES, P.80, 81, 82

Below: artworks at Dublinia portray the city's Viking history.

Central Core, South of the Liffey

Forming the heart of the city south of the River Liffey, this is where the hoards of tourists that travel to Dublin every year are at their most noticeable. There's an energetic vibe that radiates out from College Green, where Trinity College seems to act as a mediator between the affluent shopping precinct of Grafton Street and the famed Temple Bar, with its maze of cobbled streets, which are dominated by late-night pubs and bars packed to the gills with party revellers.

BORDERING THE RIVER LIFFEY

Sandwiched between Dame Street and the River Liffey, **Temple Bar** ① takes its name from Anglo-Irish aristocrat Sir William Temple, who owned the land in the 17th century when the area flourished with commercial activity. As a result of the changing level of the River Liffey, the docks area had to be moved eastwards, forcing Temple Bar into decline. In the 1980s derelict properties were leased to artists, musicians and artisans, who formed a lobbying group to fight for preservation of these buildings. It was their success that led to Temple Bar carving itself into a

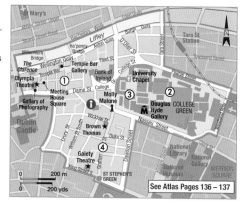

Below: the beloved Ha'penny Bridge is a city landmark.

vibrant cultural and entertainment quarter.

Today pedestrianised streets are alive with entertainers, and public open spaces such as **Meeting House Square** are the focus for artistic talent and a lively Saturday market. Dubliners believe that Temple Bar has gone over the top with tourist-orientated bars, although this would appear to have been tamed with the banning of stag and hen parties. Undeniably, Temple Bar still rocks at night, but during the day it's an atmospheric quarter, great for people-watching.

Venues such as the **Gallery of Photography** and **Temple Bar Gallery and Studios** continue to promote a cultural theme, and decent eating options abound. **The Clarence**, one of Dublin's best-known hotels, is in Temple Bar. Owned by Dublin's beloved Bono of U2 fame, some of its rooms offer lovely views over the water.

A short walk further east along the river is the **Ha'penny Bridge**, one of Dublin's most cherished landmarks.

SEE ALSO ARCHITECTURE, P.29; HOTELS, P.67; MUSEUMS AND GALLERIES, P.82, 84

Left: the *Sphere within Sphere* sculpture in the grounds of Trinity College.

Street ④, Dublin's premier shopping precinct that lays claim to the city's swankiest shops. A bronze statue of **Molly Malone** – or the 'Tart with the Cart' as she is more affectionately known – greets visitors at the north end. Street performers of all kinds create a jolly atmosphere, while flower stalls by the roadside produce a blaze of colour.

About halfway up Grafton Street, the **Brown Thomas** department store deservedly takes pride of place, and a bit further on is the mosaic facade of one of Dublin's institutions, **Bewley's Oriental Café**. Exploring the streets that criss-cross Grafton Street uncovers a hive of shops, cafés and pubs.

SEE ALSO BARS AND CAFÉS, P.32; SHOPPING, P.109; STATUES AND MONUMENTS, P.115

COLLEGE GREEN

The traffic-congested expanse of College Green is dominated by **Trinity College** ②, the most imposing assemblage of buildings in the city. Enter the gates to Ireland's most prestigious university and a whole new tranquil world opens up before you, starting with the vast square marked by Arnoldo Pomodoro's bronze sculpture *Sphere within Sphere*. A stroll around the extensive grounds is very rewarding, and the College is home to the **Douglas Hyde Gallery**, one of the country's leading contemporary galleries, but the highlight of Trinity must be a visit to the **Old Library and the Book of Kells** ③.

Across College Green, facing Trinity College, is another striking building that has been home to the **Bank of Ireland** since 1802. This grand Palladian structure was purpose-built for the Irish Parliament in 1739. One of the adjoining buildings is now occupied by the relaunched **National Wax Museum**, which moved here in 2009.

SEE ALSO ARCHITECTURE, P.30; MUSEUMS AND GALLERIES, P.82, 83

GRAFTON STREET AND AROUND

Snaking uphill from College Green is **Grafton**

Below: Temple Bar is packed with lively pubs.

Thin Lizzy guitarist Phil Lynott is immortalised in a life-size bronze statue erected on Henry Street, just off Grafton Street, nicknamed the 'Ace with the Bass'. This was considered to be a poignant place given that Phil was regularly spotted around Grafton Street visiting the flower stalls. Thin Lizzy band members attended the unveiling ceremony and paid tribute by giving a live performance. Although born in Birmingham, Lynott was raised by his grandmother on Dublin's south side and was an ambassador for Irish rock. In his last years he was dogged by drug and alcohol dependency, and his death on 4 January 1986 aged 36 was a great loss to Dublin.

St Stephen's Green and Around

One of the most famous areas in Dublin and most noted for its superb Georgian architecture, St Stephen's Green was *the* address to have in the 18th century. Favoured by the beaux of the day to strut their stuff, it still retains its cachet, with the Shelbourne Hotel on the north side of the square boasting the 'best address in Dublin'. Take a drink in the bar at the hotel and you can do some modern-day celebrity-spotting. The park in the centre of the square is the perfect spot to escape from the crowds.

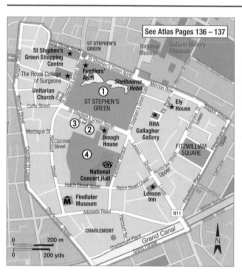

See Atlas Pages 136 – 137

Above: the Wolfe Tone memorial.

ON THE GREEN

Office workers, shop assistants and tourists alike seek the refuge of the 9-hectare (22-acre) **St Stephen's Green** ①, an oasis of green in the centre of the city. In the early 17th century the park was just a marshy common for grazing cattle. It was enclosed with a wall in 1664 and buildings erected around its perimeter, but still hosted public hangings. Notorious for crime, it wasn't until the houses were demolished

and the spanking new Georgian townhouses were built that it began to assume a more genteel air. Most of the present-day park is Victorian in layout. Entering by the northwest corner, pass through the **Fusiliers' Arch**, a monument to soldiers of the Boer War, and into the park, passing the lakes with waterfowl, on to the central formal garden and the bandstand. Notable monuments in the park are the **Three Fates Fountain**

and the modern memorial to nationalist Wolfe Tone, which is known locally as **Tonehenge**.
SEE ALSO PARKS AND GARDENS, P.97; STATUES AND MONUMENTS, P.114

BUILDINGS AROUND THE GREEN

Taking a stroll around the Green, there are several buildings to look out for. St Stephen's Green North is home to the **Shelbourne Hotel**, a meeting place for high society since 1824. South of the Green is **Iveagh House**, once home to the Guinness family, who donated it to the State in 1939; it now houses the offices of the Irish Department of Foreign Affairs.

Left: the upmarket Shelbourne Hotel.

fort Terrace, is the **National Concert Hall**, originally built for the Dublin International Exhibition of 1865 and home to RTÉ National Symphony Orchestra.

To the east of St Stephen's Green, in Ely Place, is the **RHA Gallagher Gallery**. The gallery was built in 1988 and, despite its incongruity among its Georgian neighbours, provides a discreet, airy space for exhibitions.

Continuing eastwards is **Fitzwilliam Square**, one of Dublin's most famous squares and with architecture spanning all four Georgian kings. Come here for the Georgian detail, the delightful fanlights over the pretty coloured doors, the original doorknockers and elaborate iron footscrapers. The gardens are private and for resident key-holders only.
SEE ALSO ARCHITECTURE, P.28; MUSEUMS AND GALLERIES, P.84; MUSIC, P.90; PARKS AND GARDENS, P.96

Further along is **Newman House** ②, which is among the most handsome of Georgian houses in Dublin. It's easy to miss the **University Church** ③ next door, its plain entrance belying the wonderful Byzantine-style interior.

Turning into St Stephen's Green West, the striking **Royal College of Surgeons** building can be seen about halfway up, a glorious memorial to Georgian architecture at its best. Built in 1806, it has a

Below: a waterfall in the lovely Iveagh Gardens.

neoclassical granite facade and distinctive round-headed windows. Check out the three statues above the pediment – Hygieia (goddess of health), Asclepius (god of medicine) and Athena (goddess of wisdom).
SEE ALSO ARCHITECTURE, P.30; CHURCHES, P.43

BEYOND THE GREEN

South of St Stephen's Green are the lovely, less known **Iveagh Gardens** ④. Beyond Iveagh House, which is not open to the public, the gardens lie hidden from view. There are two entrances, one on Clonmel Street and one on Hatch Street. It may well prove the perfect spot to eat lunch on a warm summer's day when St Stephen's Green is overrun with picnickers.

Close to Iveagh Gardens, with its entrance on Earls-

During the 1916 Easter Rising members of the Irish Citizen Army, led by Michael Mallin and Countess Markiewicz, occupied St Stephen's Green. They established roadblocks and dug defensive positions in the park. This proved their downfall as snipers from the British army took up positions in the Shelbourne Hotel and shot at the insurgents down in the park. As they retreated to the Royal College of Surgeons, the gunfire continued, and you can still see the bullet holes in the pillars of the building. Incredibly, gunfire was temporarily halted to allow park staff to feed the ducks.

Georgian District and Museums

This is Dublin at its most grandiose, the heart of the cultural and governmental quarter. There is surely something for everyone here – museum buffs, architectural gurus, lovers of green spaces and those who just like to soak up the ambience of a special city. Clustered together are some of the finest institutions in Europe, housed in the most splendid of Georgian and Victorian architectural masterpieces. Keep an eye open for the Georgian details on the townhouses, from fanlights to door-scrapers.

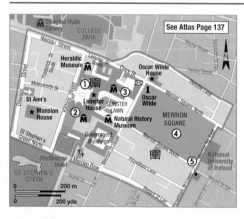

See Atlas Page 137

Above: a distinctively Georgian-district front door.

GOVERNMENT AND MUSEUM DISTRICT

The district bordered by Clare Street to the north and Merrion Row to the south contains the grandest buildings in Dublin. **Leinster House** was built in 1745 and now accommodates both Houses of the Irish Parliament, the Dail and the Senate. Tours can be taken when Parliament is not sitting, or you can sit in the Public Gallery when the House is in session.

On either side of Leinster House are the Irish **National Library** ① and the **National Museum of Ireland, Archaeology** ②, both fine examples of mid-

Victorian architecture. The National Museum has a superb collection displayed in magnificent surroundings and also offers a pleasant café.

Moving on towards Merrion Square are two further Dublin institutions, the **Natural History Museum** (closed until further notice) and the **National Gallery of Ireland** ③, one of Europe's finest art galleries.

SEE ALSO ARCHITECTURE, P.29, 30, 31; MUSEUMS AND GALLERIES, P.84, 85

AROUND MERRION SQUARE

The epitome of Georgian town planning, **Merrion**

Square ④ was laid out by Lord Fitzwilliam of Merrion in the 1770s and names among its illustrious residents Oscar Wilde, who lived at No. 1, Daniel O'Connell at No. 58 and W. B. Yeats at No. 82. Wilde's languishing **statue** can be seen within the park in the square, along with a charming sculpture of a pregnant woman, representing his wife Constance, and also a sculpture of a male torso.

Just to the southeast of Merrion Square is the

Born at 21 Westland Row in Dublin, Oscar Wilde (1854–1900), the son of wealthy professional parents, moved to Merrion Square in 1855, where he resided until 1878. He attended Trinity College from 1871 until 1874, proving a first-class scholar and gaining a scholarship to Oxford. After graduation he returned to Dublin and married Constance Lloyd in 1884; they subsequently settled in Tite Street, London. His novels and plays, including *The Picture of Dorian Gray* (1890) and *The Importance of Being Earnest* (1895), were a great success and he became one of the biggest celebrities of the day. However, his downfall came as a result of sexual scandal and he was imprisoned for homosexuality. He died in Paris in 1900, alone and poor. *See also Literature, p.76.*

Georgian gem **Number 29** ⑤, a must for lovers of the 18th century. Number 29 reveals the life of the upper echelons of Dublin society and reproduces a harmonious design, one of luxury and grace. Bear in mind that much of Dublin suffered from high rates of crime and deprivation; the streets around Merrion Square may well have been of a high social standing, but not far away squalor and poverty abounded.

SEE ALSO ARCHITECTURE, P.28, 30; MUSEUMS AND GALLERIES, P.86; PARKS AND GARDENS, P.97; STATUES AND MONUMENTS, P.114

CHURCH AND STATE

Two buildings on Dawson Street epitomise the smart side of Church and State in this elegant district of the city. **St Ann's Church** never wanted for benefactors as it was central to the society of the nearby

newly designed Georgian squares and streets. The charitable work of local residents lives on in a bequest of 1723 made by Baron Butler that 120 loaves of bread each week to be left on a shelf for the poor, which is still upheld today. Nationalist leader Wolfe Tone and Dracula creator Bram Stoker were both married

Below: the Georgian National Gallery of Ireland.

at St Ann's. For the best view of the church, look down Anne Street South from Grafton Street.

The second building of note in Dawson Street is the **Mansion House**. It has been the official residence of Lord Mayor of Dublin since 1715. It was here, in the Round Room, on 21 January 1919, that the first Irish Parliament proclaimed the Irish Declaration of Independence. Dawson Street is lined with restaurants and bars, and, although the Mansion House is closed to the public, part of the building is now a business and events centre, and houses the restaurant **Fire**.

SEE ALSO CHURCHES, P.43; RESTAURANTS, P.104

Docklands and Canals

Dublin's dockland and canal districts portray several very different images that blend harmoniously into one – from historic grand buildings standing on the quayside to a regenerated docklands, immersed in glass, concrete and steel, and the tranquil Grand Canal towpath that offers a perfect escape from the city madness. In the rejuvenation of Docklands and Grand Canal Dock, Dublin is looking to the future. Focusing on the existing natural elements, the city has formulated a new trend of apartments, offices, hotels, shops and eating and cultural venues that cater to the Dubliners and sightseers of tomorrow.

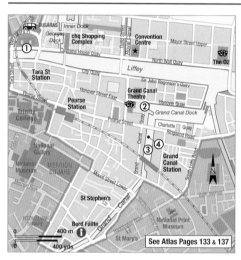

Above: the *Jeanie Johnston* tall ship replica.

CUSTOM HOUSE QUAY

Despite the transformation going on around Customs House Quay, the majestic **Custom House** ① has managed to stand its ground here on the waterfront for over 200 years. One of the most outstanding examples of James Gandon's work, the structure stretches 114m (374ft) along the embankment and is a formidable sight. A Continental-style boardwalk follows the river in front of the Custom House, where the emaciated *Famine Figures* stand, commemorating the Great Famine of 1845. Near here is the boarding point for the **Liffey River Cruise**. Further along, a recreation of the 19th-century *Jeanie Johnston* tall ship is moored beside the quay – unless it's out at sea serving its principal function as a training vessel.

Across the road opposite, Georges Dock and its central pontoon are the focal point for a growing number of events that take place here. Beside Georges Dock is a converted 19th-century tobacco store; the former vaults below are still visible at the front of the building. It now houses the **chq** shopping and eating complex, where retail space is starting to fill up with upmarket individual shops. Back behind is Inner Dock, where the former Dockmaster's Office, dating from 1820, still stands.
SEE ALSO ARCHITECTURE, P.28; STATUES AND MONUMENTS, P.115; WALKS, BUS TOURS AND BOAT TRIPS, P.127

NORTH WALL QUAY

As Custom House Quay

It is said that a Dubliner is only a true Dubliner if born within the confines of the city's two canals: the Grand Canal, which meanders for 6km (4 miles), looping around the south side and the Royal Canal, which takes a similar course north of the city.

merges into North Wall Quay, the cylindrical glass atrium of the **Convention Centre** (opening 2010) is rapidly becoming an iconic landmark among the urban apartments and offices. Trendy cafés are moving in to serve the growing number of business-people working and living in this area.

Apart from **The 02** music venue, which stands isolated at the far end, things mostly descend into a building site from here on. Future plans include stunning new landmarks

that will pierce the skyline, further shops and cafés at Point Village and a Luas extension that will facilitate the additional amenities.
SEE ALSO MUSIC, P.92

GRAND CANAL DOCK

Grand Canal Dock has taken on a futuristic image with steel and tinted-glass tower blocks looming over what is one of the city's most innovative projects,

Left: by the banks of the Grand Canal.

Grand Canal Square ②.

Set to become the cultural and business epicentre of the city, an impressive diamond-shaped theatre (due to open in 2010) takes centre stage. Red resin-glass paving covered with red glowing light sticks stretch down to the water's edge crossed by a green carpet of polygon-shaped planters and seating; after dark the square is a mass of illuminations. With many eating and drinking options, the wharf-like setting is a hub of activity both day and night.

GRAND CANAL

The regeneration of Grand Canal Dock has progressed towards the **Grand Canal** ③; here many of the 18th-century stone buildings have been preserved from a time when the canal was an important means of transport. The white cube in the middle of the canal basin is the **Waterways Visitor Centre** ④, which gives a fascinating insight into the history of Dublin's inland waterways.

A peaceful stroll along the towpath that stretches from Mount Street Lower and Leeson Street is a highlight of a visit to Dublin. Take a few minutes to sit on the bench beside the bronze statue of **Patrick Kavanagh** and watch the world go by.
SEE ALSO MUSEUMS AND GALLERIES, P.86; STATUES AND MONUMENTS, P.115

Left: a statue of Patrick Kavanagh looks out over the Grand Canal.

17

North of the Liffey, West

Northwest of the centre, this predominantly residential district is less visited by tourists than most other parts of Dublin. Those that do come are normally here for the Old Jameson Distillery in Smithfield, which is at the centre of an urban renewal scheme where the old rubs shoulders with the new. This is where Dublin's legal quarter can be found, evident by the number of bigwig barristers milling around the area. Venturing further north is rewarded with some delightful green retreats and the leafy suburb of Glasnevin, with its fascinating cemetery and world-renowned botanical gardens.

AROUND SMITHFIELD

Smithfield ① is one of the oldest parts of Dublin and has been associated with markets and a bustling horse fair since the 17th century. More recently, this run-down quarter was targeted for redevelopment that has initiated the building of plush apartment blocks and commercial units. Restored antique cobblestones were relaid to form a huge central plaza that is lit by gigantic gas braziers. The horse market moved north to make way for high-profile concerts and other events; the original ambitious intentions to create a tourist hotspot with trendy bars and restaurants are yet to materialise.

The **Old Jameson Distillery** ② buildings occupy a large area on the western edge of Smithfield, and the tour is very popular with whiskey fans. For a 360-degree panoramic vista, take the lift up the former distillery chimney, built in 1895. The two-tiered glass-viewing platform stands at a height of 56m (185ft).

Just around the corner on Church Street, the vaults of **St Michan's Church** conceal what must be one of the most macabre sights to be found in Dublin, some very well-preserved mummies.

Above: Irish whiskey for sale.

SEE ALSO CHURCHES, P.43; MUSEUMS AND GALLERIES, P.86

GANDON LANDMARKS

James Gandon has left his mark on the cityscape here by way of the **Four Courts** ③, which have administered law and order in Ireland since 1786. It is hard to miss this imposing structure occupying a prime spot on the north bank of the River Liffey. The Four

Glasnevin Cemetery is the main Catholic cemetery in Dublin. Before it was opened in 1832 there were no specifically Roman Catholic graveyards in the city due to the Penal Laws imposed by the British authorities, restricting the civil rights of Catholics and Presbyterians. In 1825, the funeral procession of Catholic John D'Arcy was met at the gate of St Kevin's Cemetery, which was under the authority of the Protestant Archbishop of Dublin, and told that Catholic prayers were forbidden from being recited at the graveside. A huge outcry erupted, and Daniel O'Connell used the scandal to push through the legislation that established Prospect Cemetery.

Left: Glasnevin Cemetary.

NORTHERN RETREATS

Just a bit further on from the King's Inns, north up Constitution Hill, is one of Dublin's best-kept secrets, **Blessington Street Basin**. City-dwellers and visitors who have discovered this idyllic spot find it hard to comprehend that they are only a 10-minute stroll away from the noisy city centre.

Continue to the residential neighbourhood of **Glasnevin**, 3km (2 miles) north of the city centre. Glasnevin was built on the former site of a monastery and is mostly known for its two well-wooded neighbours that are divided by a stone wall – the **National Botanic Gardens** and **Glasnevin Cemetery** ④. Glasnevin Cemetery, also known as Prospect Cemetery, is the final resting place of many prominent figures who have helped shape Ireland's past and can take a few hours to explore properly.
SEE ALSO PARKS AND GARDENS, P.98

Courts also played a part in the Civil War, when Republican forces occupied the building in 1922 protesting against the Anglo-Irish Treaty. After a week of being besieged from across the river by Treaty supporters led by Michael Collins, the building suffered severe fire damage and had to be rebuilt in 1932. These events marked the start of the Civil War.

Another example of Gandon's work is the honourable society of the **King's Inns**, the oldest institution of its kind in Ireland. Steeped in tradition dating back to 1541, it is amid these admired surroundings that Ireland's future barristers are trained. Famous graduates of the King's Inns include arguably the greatest

leader of Catholic Ireland, Daniel O'Connell, Theobald Wolfe Tone, described as the founder of Irish Nationalism, and Patrick Pearse, who was executed for delivering the Proclamation of Independence.
SEE ALSO ARCHITECTURE, P.29

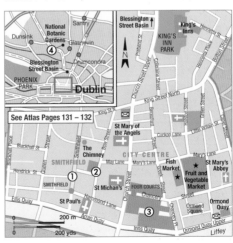

Left: Smithfield has seen extensive regeneration.

O'Connell Street
and Beyond

Traditionally not thought of as a tourist district, the much-smartened-up O'Connell Street and its environs have plenty to attract visitors and locals alike. Shopping is well catered for with splendid malls, as well as the vibrant Moore Street Market, where traders can still be found selling fruit and vegetables from old prams, while the new Quartier Bloom, with its cafés and Italian delis, has a Continental feel. Steeped in history, the area's theatres, museums and charming gardens all have a story to tell.

ALONG O'CONNELL STREET

This famous thoroughfare is prominent in the development of the history of Dublin, from the statue of **Daniel O'Connell** at its south end to the monument of **Charles Stewart Parnell** at the north end. These fighters for Ireland's freedom paved the way for the final Republican showdown at the **General Post Office** ①, located on the left walking north. Known as the GPO, this atmospheric building saw the bloodiest siege of the 1916 Easter Rising. It was here that the reading of the Proclamation of the Irish Republic took place, but the insurgents

Below: the Spire looms over O'Connell Street.

were forced to surrender after the interior was reduced to rubble, and 16 rebels were later executed.

Just beyond here, and impossible to miss, is the gleaming **Spire**, stretching way up into the sky. Glancing across the street you will see **Clery's** department store and its famous **clock**. Further on north up O'Connell Street is the **Gresham**, one of Dublin's grandest hotels, built in 1817.
SEE ALSO HOTELS, P.72; SHOPPING, P.109; STATUES AND MONUMENTS, P.114, 115

OFF O'CONNELL STREET, EAST

At the south end of O'Connell Street with the river behind, the first turning on the right is Abbey Street, where you will find the famous **Abbey Theatre**, founded in 1903. A little further north of here is Earl Street, which is home to a statue of one of Ireland's greatest novelists, **James Joyce**. In Marlborough Street, left off Earl Street, you will find **St Mary's Pro-Cathedral**, where Joyce used to worship.

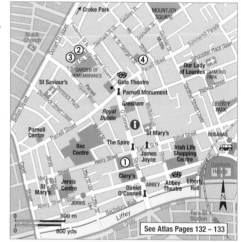

Left: in the Dublin Writers Museum in Parnell Square.

greatest of all Dublin's Georgian squares and the most sought-after place to live. Its subsequent demise saw a decline in the area, and many properties fell into disrepair. Fortunately most houses have been restored to their former glory, and once again it is a desirable spot to visit, with an attractive park at its centre.

Travelling further north, passing over the Royal Canal you are confronted by the formidable structure of **Croke Park**, home to the Gaelic Athletic Association and the **GAA Museum**.

SEE ALSO MUSEUMS AND GALLERIES, P.87, 88, 89; PARKS AND GARDENS, P.98, 99; SPORTS, P.112; STATUES AND MONUMENTS, P.114; THEATRE AND DANCE, P.117

Left: the bloom-decorated statue of James Joyce.

desirable in the 18th century. The square itself is now home to the **Dublin Writers Museum** ② and the **Dublin City Gallery, The Hugh Lane** ③. Set in the centre of the square is the poignant **Garden of Remembrance**, a peaceful green oasis featuring the *Children of Lír* monument.

South of the square, the **Gate Theatre** has been a mainstay of Irish culture since the early 20th century. To the east, in North Great George's Street, further complementing this area of literary prowess, is the **James Joyce Centre** ④, a shrine to the great man of Irish literature.

Heading northeast you come to **Mountjoy Square**, at one time the

SEE ALSO CHURCHES, P.42; STATUES AND MONUMENTS, P.115; THEATRE AND DANCE, P.116

AROUND PARNELL SQUARE AND BEYOND

The area around Parnell Square, at the top end of O'Connell Street, was one of the grandest and most

Daniel O'Connell (1775–1847), also known as 'The Liberator', was born in County Kerry into a once-wealthy Roman Catholic family who had become dispossessed. A wealthy uncle put Daniel through education and he studied law firstly in London and then at King's Inns, Dublin. From an early age he immersed himself in the rights of his countrymen; he was a passionate advocate of religious tolerance and succeeded in instigating the Catholic Emancipation Act of 1829. Following a short imprisonment for sedition in 1844 and conflict with authority he left Ireland in 1847, dying shortly afterwards. Sackville Street was renamed O'Connell Street in 1924 in memory of him.

Ballsbridge and Around

It is a great shame that the majority of visitors to Dublin never venture southeast of the Grand Canal to Ballsbridge – unless they are in town for the rugby or a horse show. Only a short bus journey from the city centre, a visit to the city's stockbroker belt provides a different perspective on Dublin. Georgian terraces fade into grand detached villas set back on broad boulevards, creating a much more relaxed atmosphere. There are good hotel and bed-and-breakfast options, and an additional plus is the close proximity of the seafront at Sandymount, the perfect antidote to the hustle and bustle of the city.

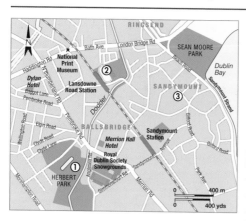

Above: the upmarket Dylan Hotel in Ballsbridge.

BALLSBRIDGE

With one of the most envied postcodes in Dublin, Ballsbridge was mainly laid out in the mid-19th century and retains some imposing architecture reflecting its affluent beginnings, an affluence that is still very evident today in its well-heeled residents. Straight,

Ballsbridge takes its name from the three-arched stone bridge spanning the River Dodder called 'Balls Bridge'. Built in 1791, the bridge replaced the original one that the Corporation built in the 1630s after an alderman was drowned crossing the river.

wide boulevards are planted with mature trees that display beautiful foliage in varying shades. Elegant Victorian and Edwardian villas adorned with ornate iron railings and brightly coloured doors are set in extensive gardens where palm trees and topiary thrive. Many of these villas are occupied by embassies that have now established themselves in Ballsbridge, along with smart hotels like the **Dylan** and good-quality bed-and-breakfasts housed in dignified ivy-clad buildings like **Merrion Hall**. There are plenty of good restaurants to be found, such as the **Lobster Pot**

and **Roly's** – frequented by residents and customers of the smart hotels.

Herbert Park ① is a delightful feature and a good example of how a relatively small park can provide a variety of amenities while at the same time fulfilling its role as a green oasis in the heart of the city. The central duck pond was constructed for the Dublin International Trades Exhibition (a kind of mini World Fair), which was held on the site in 1907 prior to it becoming a public park.

Ballsbridge is also home to the **Royal Dublin Society Showgrounds**, which were set up here in 1879. This huge area with

Left: Lansdowne Road Stadium, the home of Irish rugby.

Early December sees the year's biggest craft fair come to town. Held at the RDS in Ballsbridge, the work of over 500 Irish artists, designers and craftspeople fills the stands. Thousands of people pass through the doors looking for unique gifts for Christmas. You never know, you might be buying from the next Paul Costelloe or John Rocha!

SANDYMOUNT

Within walking distance from Ballsbridge beyond Lansdowne Road, is the coastal suburb of Sandymount ③, which has two very distinct parts. In the small village, cafés, restaurants and Art Nouveau shop fronts are set around a triangular park with a bust of **W. B. Yeats** at the centre. Like neighbouring Ballsbridge, Sandymount is also an affluent area with many large houses that mostly date back to the 19th and early 20th centuries.

its tended turf, white fences and striking buildings covers 16 hectares (40 acres) and is where the prestigious **Dublin Horse Show** takes place every August. The complex is used regularly for other events and exhibitions, and the concert hall attracts top international stars to its stage; in 1981 and 1988 the Eurovision Song Contest took place here.

Looming in the background is a landmark worshipped by many a devoted Dubliner – the reconstructed home of the national rugby team, the **Lansdowne Road Stadium** ②. The original stadium served the **IRFU** (Irish Rugby Football Union) from 1876, when the first international rugby match was played.

Between Lansdowne Road and the Grand Canal is the **National Print Museum**, an enlightening museum often overshadowed by the major ones in the city centre.

SEE ALSO FESTIVALS AND EVENTS, P.55; HOTELS, P.72; RESTAURANTS, P.107; SPORTS, P.113

A short walk away is **Sandymount Strand**. The sea goes out for miles here, exposing a large expanse of sand where, on a sunny day, you will see children playing ball games or gathering crabs from the pockets of water that settle further out. It is a pleasant walk along the promenade that runs along the coast road, or you can take a stroll around the headland, from where the ferries leaving the port at Dún Laoghaire are visible in the distance. Sandymount has its own DART station.

Left: Sandymount Strand.

23

Beyond Dublin

One of the great things about a trip to cosmopolitan Dublin is just how easy it is to take a break from the city and sample something of the 'real' Ireland. Take a short trip on the DART to taste the sea air and blow away the city cobwebs. Within an hour or so of Dublin there are some first-class attractions. For superb gardens visit Powerscourt, for early Irish history Brú na Bóinne, for crafts and village ambience Avoca, for horses the Kildare stud, and for peace and quiet, walking and sheer beauty, be sure not to miss Glendalough and the Wicklow Mountains. So do consider a few days out of the city to sample the Irish country hospitality.

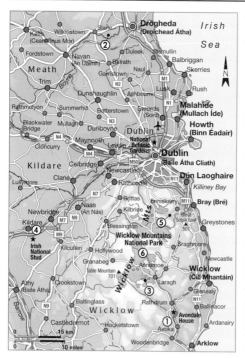

TV series *Ballykissangel*, which put it on the tourist trail. The main reason, however, people come to Avoca is to buy the superb high-quality cashmere and mohair products. You can visit the weaving shed, shop and excellent café at the **Old Mill** on the edge of the village. Many of the throws, rugs and scarves you'll find in Avoca stores are woven here. Admission is free, and it is a great opportunity to see a working mill before visiting the factory shop.

BRÚ NA BÓINNE ②
Brú na Bóinne (Palace of the Boyne), a UNESCO World Heritage Site, is located in County Meath. The **Visitor Centre** at Brú na Bóinne introduces and interprets the incredible Neolithic monuments of Newgrange, Nowth and Dowth, the great tombs that are some 5,000 years old and predate the Egyptian pyramids. The site covers 780 hectares (1,927 acres) and contains around 40 passage graves, high round mounds raised over stone burial chambers.

OUT ON THE DART
You can easily get out and about along the coast on the light rail DART, be it for visiting attractions or strolling along one of the long sandy beaches. There are stations to the north and south; stops that each offer a different slant on suburban life in Dublin.
SEE ALSO DART EXCURSIONS, P.44; TRANSPORT, P.123

AVOCA ①
Avoca has two claims to fame, firstly as a backdrop for the popular 1990s BBC

Right: in Avoca.

Left: Powerscourt Gardens back onto stunning scenery.

Powerscourt. Outdoor highlights include the Italian terraced gardens, the lovely 18th-century walled garden, the 1908 **Japanese Garden** and the cascading **Powerscourt Waterfall**, which at 121m (398ft) is the highest in Ireland. Inside the house there is a visual history of the estate and an Avoca café and store. The former estate glasshouses now contain the **Powerscourt Garden Pavilion**.

WICKLOW MOUNTAINS NATIONAL PARK ⑥

The Wicklow Mountains National Park has a total extent of 20,483 hectares (50,613 acres) and covers most of County Wicklow with terrain as diverse as lakes, high granite moors and wooded valleys. The highest point is **Lugnaquilla** at 925m (3,035ft). You can learn more about the park and its extensive flora and fauna at the **Visitor Centre** at Glendalough.

In 1690, the Battle of the Boyne took place on opposing sides of the River Boyne, around 3km (2 miles) north of the village of Donore, and saw deposed Catholic King James II defeated by the Protestant King William of Orange, who went on to secure the crown of Great Britain. The battle was primarily about James's attempt to regain the thrones of England and Scotland and was the result of Parliament's move to put William on the throne, but is primarily remembered as a crucial moment in the struggle between Irish Protestant and Catholic interests. A Visitor Centre at the site gives more information.

GLENDALOUGH ③

For sheer beauty in a magical setting, you can't beat this wonderful monastic settlement deep in the **Wicklow Mountains**. **Glendalough** (Valley of the Two Lakes) is one of the best-preserved religious sites in Ireland and was founded by St Kevin in AD570. Despite being one of the most visited places in Ireland, the peace and serenity is tangible, the surrounding countryside sub-

lime. The excellent modern Visitor Centre interprets the buildings and the history surrounding the site.

KILDARE ④

The low-lying countryside of County Kildare is ideal horse-racing territory, and anyone interested in horses can visit the **Irish National Stud**, just outside Kildare town. There are guided tours of the paddocks and stables and a chance to visit the **Horse Museum**. Visit between February and July for the best chance of seeing foals. For garden buffs, close by are the delightful **Japanese Gardens** and the contemplative **St Fiachra's Garden**.

POWERSCOURT HOUSE AND GARDENS ⑤

A combination of mountain backdrop, architectural grandeur and stunning formal gardens greet you at

A–Z

In the following section Dublin's attractions and services are organised by theme, under alphabetical headings. Items that link to another theme are cross-referenced. All sights that are plotted on the atlas section at the end of the book are given a page number and grid reference.

Architecture

At first glance you might think that there was not much of architectural interest in Dublin other than the fabulous array of 18th-century Georgian buildings – from gracious townhouses in delectable squares to grandiose institutions. James Gandon, who produced the epitome of Georgian style, designed many of these. If you look further, however, you will find medieval churches, monumental Victorian museums and modest warehouses, slick office complexes and dockland conversions. Throw in a few interesting bridges and some ornate decoration and Dublin reveals itself to be a melting pot of architectural interest.

GEORGIAN ARCHITECTURE

Dublin simply heaves with Georgian gems. To catch a glimpse of a large number of the best, go to the **St Stephen's Green** and **Merrion Square** districts. Around these squares, and others such as **Fitzwilliam Square** to the south, are some glorious examples of Georgian townhouses.

The beauty is in the detail – take a good look at the panelled front doors, the ornate semicircular fanlights above and the ironwork on the railings. Even the coalholes in the pavement had decorative covers. Between Kildare Street and Merrion Square you will find the height of Georgian grandeur with imposing government buildings, such

as **Leinster House**. Fine examples of later Georgian architecture include the exquisite **Royal College of Surgeons** building on St Stephen's Green West and the magnificent **General Post Office** building in O'Connell Street.

SEE ALSO PARKS AND GARDENS, P.97

JAMES GANDON

Londoner James Gandon (1743–1823) played a huge part in the development of Georgian architecture in the city. He arrived in Dublin by a quirk of fate. About to leave to work in St Petersburg, he was invited by Lord Carlow to oversee the building of the new **Custom House** (1791) in Dublin after the original architect, Thomas Cooley, died. Completed for the then-vast expense of £200,000, the project was unpopular with Dublin taxpayers, but the stunning

Left: a typical front door in Dublin's Georgian style.

Left: the imposing Four Courts building.

land.ie; May–late Sept daily 10am–5pm (guided tours only); admission charge; bus: 20A, 27, 42; DART: Clontarf Road

Designed by George III's architect Sir William Chambers (1723–96), this delightful casino or 'small house' is regarded as one of the finest neoclassical buildings in Ireland. It was designed for Lord Charlemont as a garden pavilion at his Marino estate. Today it is surrounded by modern suburbia, but imagined in its former rural setting it must have resembled a delightful Roman temple. It looks deceptively small from the outside, but inside are 16 rooms, many beautifully decorated with fine ornamental plasterwork.

Leinster House

Kildare Street; tel: 01 618 3166; visits by prior arrangement when Parliament not in session; free; bus: 10a, 14a, 15a; DART: Pearse; map p.137 D3

Above: Gandon's O'Connell Bridge.

design was the turning point in Gandon's career and he settled in Dublin.

Although the Custom House is closed to the public, it is especially splendid when viewed from across the River Liffey. Gandon went on to design the Carlisle Bridge (now known as **O'Connell Bridge**) and the striking **Four Courts** (1796) to be found along the Liffey at Inns Quay. This building can be visited only when courts are in session.

Another venerable and beautiful Gandon building is **King's Inns** in Henrietta Street. Tours can be made by prior arrangement.

Although not the primary architect, Gandon

also made a contribution to another iconic Georgian building in the city, the **Bank of Ireland**. He added the curving and windowless screen and the east-facing Corinthian portico between 1785 and 1789, and a corresponding portico was added to the west side some years later. Other interesting Gandon projects were the pretty **Mountjoy Square** and the **Rotunda Assembly Rooms** at the top of O'Connell Street.

GEORGIAN BUILDINGS

Casino, Marino

Cherrymount Crescent, off the Malahide Road, Marino; tel: 01 833 1618; www.heritageire

So iconic is the **Ha'penny Bridge** to Dubliners, it has been recognised as the unofficial symbol of the city. Opened as the Wellington Bridge in 1816, named after the famous 'Iron Duke', it acquired its nickname from the toll of one old half penny paid up until 1919. The bridge was cast in Coalbrookdale in Shropshire. It was closed between 2001 and 2003 for renovation and was repainted in its original off-white colour, while the original line of decking was also restored. Three lamps supported by curved ironwork over the walkway make the bridge particularly attractive when illuminated at night.

Left: Leinster House *(see p.29).*

century include **Sir William Chambers' Examination Hall and Chapel**. Later buildings, including the **Naughton Institute** and **Crann Building** of 2007, are located well behind the Georgian gems.
SEE ALSO MUSEUMS AND GALLERIES, P.83

This impressive house, the seat of the Irish government, was designed in 1745 by Richard Cassells for the Earls of Kildare and Leinster of the Fitzgerald family, and built to reflect their position in society. It remained in the family for just 70 years, was sold to the Royal Dublin Society and subsequently bought by the Irish government in 1925. It's likely that architect James Hoban, who studied in Dublin, saw designs for Leinster House before he created his prize-winning plans for America's White House in Washington, DC.

Newman House
85–86 St Stephen's Green South; tel: 01 477 9810; June–end Aug Tue–Fri tours 2pm, 3pm, 4pm; bus: 14a, 15a, 128; map p.136 C2
Newman House, named after Cardinal Newman who used the house in the 1850s, is made up of two of the finest Georgian houses in Dublin. Not only are the external features delightful, the interior has superb ornamented and stuccoed walls and ceilings, some of which were decorated by the renowned Lafranchini brothers.

Oscar Wilde House
1 Merrion Square; bus: 45; DART: Pearse; map p.137 D3
Unfortunately the former home of writer Oscar Wilde is no longer open to the public. It is, however, well worth viewing from the outside for its Georgian architecture. It was the first to be built on the square in 1762, and has fine decorative cornices and architraves. Just over the road in the gardens is an amusing statue of the illustrious writer.
PARKS AND GARDENS, P.97

Trinity College
College Green; tel: 01 896 1000; Campus main gate Mon–Fri 7am–midnight, Sat–Sun and public hols 8am–6pm, college tours mid-May–Sept; campus free, tours admission charge; bus: 10a, 13a, 15a; DART: Pearse; map p.137 C4–D4
A stroll around the campus of Trinity College makes you fully appreciate the grand and varied architecture. The earliest buildings date to Georgian times, the first being Thomas Burgh's masterpiece, the **Old Library** (1712–32), which dominates the view of the university from Nassau Street. Other buildings added during the 18th

LATER ARCHITECTURE
Although Dublin is renowned for its superb Georgian architecture, there are also examples of later architecture worth seeking out. Close to the Georgian governmental buildings near Merrion Square are fine exponents of monumental Victorian architecture, the **National Museum of Ireland** (1885), **National Gallery of Ireland** (1864) and the **National Library of Ireland** (1885).
The suburbs, such as Ballsbridge, reveal some attractive Victorian and Edwardian villas, and throughout the city you will find examples of Victorian building in commercial premises and warehouses.

National Gallery of Ireland
Merrion Square West; tel: 01 661 5133; www.national gallery.ie; Mon–Sat 9.30am–5.30pm, Thur until 8.30pm, Sun noon–5.30pm; free; bus: 45; map p.137 D3
The grandiose facade of the National Gallery mimics the Natural History Museum building in Merrion Street (closed to the pubic), although its elaborate por-

Right: the James Joyce Bridge, even more striking at night.

tico was added to the original design. The building was completed in 1864.
SEE ALSO MUSEUMS AND GALLERIES, P.84

National Library
Kildare Street; tel: 01 603 0200; www.nli.ie; exhibitions: Mon–Wed 9.30am–9pm, Thur–Fri 9.30am–5pm, Sat 9.30am–4.30pm; free; bus: 15a, 74a, 92; map p.137 D3
The building's most impressive feature is the entrance rotunda, which contains an impressive staircase leading to the superb reading room with a vast vaulted celing.
SEE ALSO MUSEUMS AND GALLERIES, P.85

National Museum of Ireland, Archaeology
Kildare Street; tel: 01 677 7444; www.museum.ie; Tue–Sat 10am–5pm, Sun 2pm–5pm; free; bus: 15a, 74a, 92; map p.137 D3
Designed by father and son architects Sir Thomas Newenham Deane and Sir Thomas Manley Deane, as part of the same scheme as the National Library, the impressive museum build-

ing has a vast street frontage.
SEE ALSO MUSEUMS AND GALLERIES, P.85

MODERN ARCHITECTURE
Check out the **chq** building in the IFC district in Docklands, a stunning 1821 warehouse modernised as a shopping centre. Striking examples of ultra-modern architecture are on show at both Docklands and Grand Canal Square. Striking glass buildings with green credentials include the new stylish **Convention Centre**, designed by Irish architect Kevin Roche due to open in September 2010. Located in Spencer Dock, this iconic structure will bring a new dimension to the northern bank of the Liffey. Its central atrium contains 475 panels of glass. Behind the south bank of the river is Grand Canal Dock, with its wide-open square, and another glass creation, the **Grand Canal Theatre** designed by Daniel Libeskind, its iconic geometric shape

Since 2000 a new generation of modern bridges has been installed over the River Liffey. The **Millennium Bridge** paved the way with a footbridge designed by Howley Harrington. The **James Joyce Bridge** (2003) was designed by Santiago Calatrava and looks particularly fine at night due to its integral lighting. As the Docklands area developed the pedestrian **Sean O'Casey Bridge**, designed by Cyril O'Neill, was installed in 2005. Calatrava is also responsible for the latest Docklands bridge, the **Samuel Beckett Bridge**, which was hauled up the Liffey in May 2009 to be in place for use in 2010.

creating a superb backdrop to the square.

Grand Canal Theatre
Grand Canal Square; DART: Grand Canal Dock
To be opened in 2010, this diamond-shaped stunner is worth a visit just to marvel at its design. The dazzling glass construction creates a fine backdrop to the regenerated Grand Canal Square.

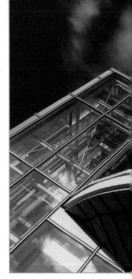

Bars and Cafés

O ne of the great pleasures of a visit to Dublin
is relaxing with a cup of your favourite
brew and watching the world go by, and there
are more than enough cafés, coffee houses and
teashops to meet this need. Although traditional
pubs in Dublin are legendary, the large numbers
of wine and cocktail bars in the city offer a
refreshing alternative and tend to attract the
city's vibrant city slickers. The borders between
bar and club are not always definable, as many
bars have live music or a DJ and also encourage
dancing. For pubs and clubs, *see also Nightlife,
p.94*, and *Traditional Pubs, p.118*.

FAR WEST AND PHOENIX PARK
Phoenix Park Tea Rooms
Phoenix Park; tel: 01 671 4431;
daily 10am–5pm; bus: 10, 25,
26; Luas: Heuston Station then
shuttle bus daily 7am–6pm
(starts 10am Sat and Sun),
departs on the hour every hour;
map p.130 A2
Dating from late Victorian
times, these pretty tea-
rooms right outside the
Zoo gates, serving organic
products, started life as
an ice-cream parlour. The
bandstand alongside is
where tea dances once
took place. A more exten-
sive lunch menu is offered
at the café in the Phoenix
Park Visitor Centre.
SEE ALSO PARKS AND GARDENS,
P.96

SOUTH OF THE LIFFEY, WEST
Gravity Bar
Guinness Storehouse, St
James's Gate; tel: 01 404 4800;
www.guinness-storehouse.com;
daily 9.30am–5pm, July–Aug
until 8pm; bus: 51b, 78a, 123;
Luas: St James's; map p.135 C3
A tour of the Guinness

The legend that is Bewley's
was stirring in 1835, when
Samuel Bewley and his son
Charles dared to break the East
India Company's monopoly by
importing nearly 3,000 chests
of tea from China. This Irish
success story ultimately led to
the foundation of one of
Ireland's most popular and
respected brands, Bewley's,
now the market leader in fresh
ground coffee in Ireland.

Storehouse culminates at
the Gravity Bar, towering
40m (132ft) atop the Storehouse, to claim a compli-
mentary pint of Guinness
while savouring the best
panoramic view of Dublin.
It's not necessary to pay
for a tour to use the bar,
but don't expect to buy a
lager – only Guinness
products are sold.
SEE ALSO MUSEUMS AND
GALLERIES, P.78

CENTRAL CORE, SOUTH OF THE LIFFEY
Bad Ass Café
9–11 Crown Alley, Temple Bar;
tel: 01 671 2596; www.badass

cafe.com; daily 11.30am–
11pm; bus: 50, 66a, 66b; map
p.136 B1
Temple Bar grew up
around this legendary
haunt where pastas,
salads and Mexican dishes
feature, but it's the best
quarter pounder in town
that really brings in the
crowd. An overhead pulley
system sends the orders
flying across the room,
distracting diners from the
sizeable portions.

Bewley's Oriental Café
78 Grafton Street; tel: 01 672
7720; www.bewleys.com;
Mon–Wed 8am–1am,

Left: Gravity Bar, at the top of the Guinness Storehouse.

vie for position or lounge on velvet sofas. It's a popular hotspot for both gay and straight crowds.

Hogans
35 South Great George's Street; tel: 01 677 5904; Mon–Wed 2pm–11.30pm, Thur until 1am, Sat until 2.30am, Sun until 11pm; bus: 16a, 19a, 83; map p.136 B3

With cold beer served at a pace by efficient staff and a lively atmosphere, Hogans is a great place to finish up a night on the town. It's mostly standing room only in the main bar, but there's a seating area on the side; the basement bar features DJs at the weekend.

Left: ornate Bewley's Oriental Café is one of the most famous cafés in Dublin.

Thur–Sat 8am–11pm, Sun 9am–10pm; bus: 10a, 14a, 70b; map p.136 C3

Dublin's most famous brand may have changed with the times, but the café's heritage is still evident in its superb roasted coffee and the oriental tearoom with stained-glass windows. Today, Bewley's offers freshly baked pastries, great sandwiches and other contemporary cuisine to go with its well-known beverages.

Dakota Bar
9 William Street South; tel: 01 672 9696; Mon–Fri noon–11.30pm, Thur until 1.30am, Fri–Sat until 2.30am, Sun 11am–11.30pm; bus 16a, 19a, 83; map p.136 B3

A breath of fresh air from rowdy Temple Bar, this chill-out bar is popular with 20-somethings who enjoy a top night out. The comfy half-moon leather couches encourage you

to settle in for the evening, and a patio takes the strain when it gets crowded.

Front Lounge
33 Parliament Street; tel: 01 670 4112; Mon–Wed noon–11.30pm, Thur–Fri noon–1.30am, Sat noon–12.30am; bus: 50, 66a, 78a; map p.136 A1

As cool as a cucumber, the Front Lounge is a venue that is very popular for kicking off a big night out. Cocktails and champagne flow while posers

Left Bank Bar
18/21 Anglesea Street; 01 671 1822; daily 10.30am–2.30am, Sun until 1am; bus: 50, 66a, 66b; map p.136 B1

What was once the Central Bank of England now houses a hip disco lounge. Moulded coins in the ceiling and gold bars on the wall are reminiscent of the building's

Below: tucking in at the Bad Ass Café.

former roots, but gold bullion and suited employees have been replaced by cocktails.

Lemon Crepe and Coffee Co.

66 William Street South; tel: 01 672 9044; Mon–Sat 8am–7.30pm, Sun 10am–6.30pm; bus: 16a, 19a, 83; map p.136 B3

This small, refreshing café has a cosmopolitan feel that reflects the trendy international food offered, the main focus being tasty crêpes, both savoury and sweet, but there's a lot more available if this doesn't take your fancy.

Market Bar

16a Fade Street; tel: 01 613 9094; www.marketbar.ie; Mon–Thur noon–11.30pm, Fri–Sat noon–12.30am, Sun 3pm–11pm; bus: 16a, 19a, 83; map p.136 B3

Beyond the cosy beer garden is a vast sky-lit space with original Victorian brick walls and iron girders that reach up to a lofty roof. There is plenty of seating, attracting large parties after work for a drink and conversation, plus the tapas are some of the best in Dublin.

Nude

21 Suffolk Street; tel: 01 672 5577; daily Mon–Fri 7.30am–8pm, Sat 8am–7.30pm, Sun 9.30am–7.30pm; bus: 10a, 13a, 15a; map p.136 C4

At the healthiest fast-food chain in town, the emphasis is on fresh organic wraps, salads, sandwiches and soup and freshly squeezed juices, all consumed at casual canteen-style tables. There are outlets scattered all over town.

No. 4 Dame Lane

4 Dame Lane; tel: 01 679 0291; daily 5pm–2.30am, Sun until 1am; bus: 10a, 13a, 15a; map p.136 B4

Don't be deceived by this sophisticated hideaway in Dublin's backstreets: if it's a quiet drink you're after you've come to the wrong place. Comfortable booths provide a sleek space to drink, but the loud music pounding out from the upper level will ensure a party mood.

Octagon Bar

The Clarence Hotel, 6–8 Wellington Quay; tel: 01 407 0800; www.the clarence.ie/octagonbar-dublin; Tue–Sat 5pm–11.30pm, Fri until 12.30pm; bus: 50, 66a, 78a; map p.136 A1

Locals, tourists and the odd celebrity rub shoulders at this plush hangout owned by superstar Bono, a place to relax over a cocktail beside the open fire under the octagon-shaped dome. The bar food is particular good, and they also serve afternoon tea between 2pm and 5.30pm.

Queen of Tarts

Cork Hill, Dame Street; tel: 01 670 7499; daily 7.30am–7pm, Sat–Sun 9am–7pm; bus: 50, 39a, 56a; map p.136 B1

The smells wafting from this quaint teashop draw people from afar to sample scrumptious pastries, cakes and sandwiches lovingly prepared by the chatty owners, Yvonne and Regina. No longer big enough to sit all their fans, the sisters have opened another branch just around the corner (Cow's Lane, Dame Street; tel: 01 633 4681; map p.136 B1).

Left: healthy and delicious fare at Nude.

Eating at the café inside the flagship Avoca store on Suffolk Street is a perfect insight into the Avoca food experience – a feast of freshly prepared food using Avoca products, which are made from the very best natural ingredients. From a rural, family-run weaving mill that started in the retail business selling rugs, clothes and Irish crafts, Avoca has come a long way since the company was founded in 1723. There are now seven stores throughout Ireland, most with cafés, and the number continues to grow. *See also Shopping, p.109.*

Above: café culture is a major part of Dublin's landscape.

ST STEPHEN'S GREEN AND AROUND
Cobblers
Leeson Lane; tel: 01 678 5945; Mon–Fri 8am–4pm; bus: 11, 78, 118; map p.137 C1
As the name suggests, an old cobbler's shop houses this café and wine bar set out over two levels. Lunchtime is busy with local businesspeople, who scramble for the outside seats in warm weather. There is a good selection of salads, pastas, pizza and sandwiches.

SamSara
La Stampa Hotel, 35 Dawson Street; tel: 01 677 4444; www.lastampa.ie/samsara; Mon–Thur noon–12.30am, Fri, Sat noon–2.30am, Sun noon–1.30am; bus: 10a, 128, 746; map p.137 C3
You'll be mingling with some of Dublin's finer-looking people at this stunning Eastern-themed café-bar with subtle lighting and a particularly impressive elevated bar. The DJ spins an eclectic mix of background music.

Solas
31 Wexford Street; tel: 01 478 0583; www.solasbars.com; daily noon–12.30am, Thur–Sat until 2.30am; bus: 16a, 19a, 83
Those looking for a chilled placed to unwind gather at this funky drinking hole for their huge choice of reasonably priced drinks, good music and good food. The long, stylish bar can get very crowded at weekends.

GEORGIAN DISTRICT AND MUSEUMS
Café en Seine
40 Dawson Street; tel: 01 667 4567; Sun–Tue 11am–12.30am, Wed–Sat 11am–3am; bus: 10a, 128, 746; map p.137 C3
Although it's been around for a while, the fabulous

Below: Parisian style at the Café en Seine.

In Dublin, last orders are called at 11.30pm Monday to Thursday, 12.30pm on Friday and Saturday and 11pm on Sunday. Punters are given an extra half an hour to sup up. Many establishments have an extended licence that allows them to serve later. It is an offence to serve alcohol to anyone under 18; the city is tough on under-age drinkers, so it is a good idea to carry ID.

Parisian interior of Café en Seine is still as amazing as ever. Stunning features include an opulent glass atrium with real trees, huge lanterns and a grand piano, and the atmosphere is simply the best.

Cocoon
Unit 2 Royal Hibernian Way, Dawson Street; tel: 01 679 6259; Mon–Wed 11am–11pm, Wed–Sat 11am–3pm; bus: 10a, 128, 746; map p.137 C3
A sanctuary for posers in the heart of Dublin's cosmopolitan shopping dis-

trict, this hip hangout supports a plush chocolate and cream colour scheme and low tables lit by small candles. It's unsurprisingly pricey, as you might expect from such a stylish joint.

DOCKLANDS AND CANALS
7 Wonders
Excise Walk, IFSC; tel: 01 672 0212; Mon–Sat 6.30am–6pm, Sun 7am–5pm; bus: 53a, 151; Luas: Mayor Square; map p.136 A4
If you're a bagel connoisseur, go to 7 Wonders for the best bagels in Dublin, using ethically sourced ingredients. The sandwiches, smoothies, coffee, teas and juices are pretty good, too. Friendly staff create a relaxing feel and provide a constant supply of newspapers.

NORTH OF THE LIFFEY, WEST
Christophe's
Duck Lane, Smithfield; tel: 01 887 4417; www.christophes

cafe.com; Mon 8am–5pm, Tue–Sat 8am–10pm; bus: 66, 83; Luas: Smithfield; map p.131 E1
Those who come to Christophe's for a casual lunch feeling particularly hungry are never disappointed. The hearty home-

Below: continue your whiskey journey at the bar at the Jameson distillery.

Left: smoking is banned indoors in bars and cafes, so alfresco tables are popular when it's dry.

14a, 46a; Luas: Abbey Street; map p.132 C1

From the black and white leather seating to the walnut bar and eclectic cocktails, Traffic is one of Dublin's most ultra-designed, yet unpretentious, lounge bars. A lively crowd gathers here before heading on to a club.

BALLSBRIDGE AND AROUND

Expresso
1 St Mary's Road, Ballsbridge; tel: 01 660 0585; Mon–Sat 7.30am–9.30pm, Sat 9am–5pm, Sun 10am–5pm; bus: 5, 7, 45

Chic light-wood tables, cream leather chairs and trendy lighting set the scene for good, interesting food. The place is always buzzing, particularly for Sunday brunch, when part of the fun is absorbing the laughter and chatting going on all around.

made fare is reasonably priced and the small courtyard outside is very pleasant on a sunny day.

O'CONNELL STREET AND BEYOND

Enoteca delle Langhe
Blooms Lane; tel: 01 888 0834; Mon–Sat noon–midnight; bus: 25a, 66a, 83; Luas: Jervis; map p.131 E1

This deli-cum-wine shop is a fabulous spot for lunch, offering delicious cold plates consumed at wooden tables with an authentic Italian feel, and with the added bonus of being able to shop for wine while you eat.

JJs Bar – Jameson
Bow Street, Smithfield; tel: 01 807 2355; daily 11.30am–5.30pm, Sun from 12.30pm; bus: 66, 83; Luas: Smithfield; map p.131 E1

After completing the Jameson distillery tour, join the sociable crowd who hang out at

this bustling bar for a dram or two, although perhaps a coffee might be more welcome.

Traffic
54 Middle Abbey Street; tel: 01 873 4800; Mon–Fri 4pm–late, Sat, Sun noon–late; bus: 10a,

Below: delicious Italian bites at Enoteca delle Langhe.

Celtic Roots and Culture

The Celts left a profound legacy that is deep-rooted in the culture of Ireland. Today this culture is more often referred to as Irish, rather than Celtic, as the Celts' influence spread throughout many parts of Europe, each region forming its own distinctive cultural heritage. In recent years there has been a revival of all things Irish, in music, art, theatre, language, food and design. These traditions are kept alive by cultural resource centres, Irish music sessions and the passing down of myths and legends.

HISTORY

The first evidence of the Celts' influence in Ireland can be traced back to the 4th century BC. Their religious rites included complex burial services, and elaborate symbolic jewellery and artefacts have been discovered. The last of the Celtic tribes to arrive in Ireland were the Gaels, who enjoyed a culture of music, art and mythology. Important sites developed, such as the Hill of Tara in County Meath, a Celtic royal centre and ultimately the seat of the High King of Ireland.

Baile Átha Cliath or 'Town of the Hurdled Ford' is the original Gaelic name for Dublin, a settlement which was further upriver than the modern-day city. A second, smaller monastic settlement closer to present-day Dublin was known as Dubh Linn or 'Black Pool' and it is here the Vikings established their trading post.

Above: a Celtic cross.

The Irish are passionate about the sport of hurling, and references to stick-and-ball games are found in ancient Irish mythology. Hurling is believed to relate to shinty, still played in Scotland, and a game called bandy, which was formerly played in England and Wales. It is thought to have come to Ireland with the Celts, and references can be found to it in 5th-century writings. To get a real taster of hurling, try to go along to a game at Croke Park. *See also Sports, p.112.*

MYTH, LEGEND AND SYMBOLISM

Prior to the introduction of Christianity by St Patrick in the 5th century AD, the symbolism and myths of the Celts laid the roots of a culture that can still be found in modern Ireland. The Celts developed a strong style that has endured to this day, made popular with the Celtic revivals of the 19th and 20th centuries. The earliest items were stunning gold necklaces, known as torcs, and twisted gold bangles. Designs popular today are based on the original Celtic stone crosses, now reproduced in silver, and the intricate knotwork jewellery, symbolising eternity. Another design is the Claddagh ring, given in friendship or worn as a wedding ring. Its design features two hands clasping a heart, sometimes surmounted with a crown. Despite its origins dating to the 17th century, it takes its design from

Left: traditional dress at an Irish Folk Festival.

The Gaelic language has seen a resurgence in recent decades and can now be seen on many road signs throughout Ireland. Two well-known words in the Irish language, 'craic' and 'céilí', have their roots in the Celtic love of language and music. Craic has no direct translation into English, as it is an overall word to describe the emotion of having a good time, through fun, laughter and storytelling. The céilí refers to a get-together, to drink, sing, dance and listen to music.

legends surrounding the early Celtic kings.

SEE ALSO IRISH DESIGN, P.74

MUSIC AND INSTRUMENTS

To many, the heart of the Celtic movement must surely be traditional Irish music. From the1960s, bands such as the **Dubliners** and the **Chieftains** popularised this music, although the purists had never gone away. Early instruments included the lyre, made of wood with strings from animals' intestines, later transformed into the Irish harp, the symbol of Ireland. The airy rasp of wooden flutes complemented the thumping of the bodhrán, a simple frame drum made of wood with animal skin stretched over the fame, which was popularised by the Chieftains.

Celtic music and Irish dance is celebrated at the Comhaltas Regional Resource Centre, part of the Culturlann na hEireann (Irish Cultural Insti-tute) in Monkstown, a suburb of Dublin.

Comhaltas Regional Resource Centre

32 Belgrave Square, Monkstown; tel: 01 280 0295; www.comhaltas.ie; some classes free, contact for times and events; bus: 46a; DART: Salthill and Monkstown

This centre is the largest group involved in the promotion and preservation of Irish traditional music, with hundreds of local branches throughout Ireland. Check out the website for the huge range of classes, performances and events going on. It also has a vast archive of Irish music recordings, books and tutorials. The promotion of traditional Irish dance and the Irish language is also at the forefront of the centre's programme.

SEE ALSO MUSIC, P.91; TRADITIONAL PUBS, P.121

Below: Celtic designs in the lawns of Dublin Castle.

Children

The image Dublin conveys as a great place to party does not immediately conjure up the idea of a child-friendly city, but the Irish welcome everyone with open arms, and that most definitely includes children. Although there are no major theme parks, there's still plenty to entertain kids – interactive museums, a good zoo, boat excursions and fun events – not to mention the option of a trip out on the DART *(see DART Excursions, p.44)* to the nearby beach. There should be no problem satisfying hungry kids; several themed restaurants and cafés provide high chairs and kids' menus, and hotels go to great lengths to cater for them.

ATTRACTIONS
The Ark
11a Eustace Street; tel: 01 670 7788; www.ark.ie; Mon–Fri 10am–4pm; admission charge for activities; bus: 50, 66a, 66b; map p.136 A1

This custom-designed cultural centre targets children aged between three and 14. Charity-funded, the organisation presents an innovative programme of events that seek to extend the imagination of children, which take place in the galleries, indoor theatre, outdoor amphitheatre or workshops.

Bram Stoker Experience
Westwood Club, Clontarf Road; tel: 01 805 7824; www.thebramsstokerdracula expeerience.com; Fri 4pm–10pm, Sat–Sun noon–10pm; admission charge; bus: 20, 27, 31, DART: Clontarf Road

A tribute to the author of the spine-chilling novel *Dracula*, Bram Stoker, who was born in the suburb of Clontarf, this imaginative, interactive attraction has the power

Above: Dublin can be great fun for little ones.

to transport suspecting visitors back in time to a world where vampires rule. It may not give you nightmares, but the effects are quite convincing.

MUSEUMS
Dublinia and the Viking World
St Michael's Hill, Christchurch; tel: 01 679 4611; www.dublinia.ie; daily 10am–5pm; admission charge;

bus: 50, 56a, 123; map p.136 A4

Having gone through major redevelopment during 2009, the brand-new Dublinia will engage your youngsters even more with its state-of-the-art interactive exhibits and reconstructions that look like the real thing. Don't miss the Viking ship in the courtyard.

SEE ALSO MUSEUMS AND GALLERIES, P.81

National Wax Museum
Foster Place, College Green; tel: 01 671 8373; daily 9.30am–7.30pm (last admission 6.45pm), see website for Sun times; admission charge; bus: 10a, 13a, 15a; map p.136 C4

The National Wax Museum is guaranteed fun for all the family, but younger children will particularly enjoy the puppet theatre, while the Chamber of Horrors awaits the older and braver children.

SEE ALSO MUSEUMS AND GALLERIES, P.83

Right: tigers at Dublin Zoo.

Left: a Viking Splash tour bus sets sail in Dublin.

Throughout the year there are always lots of different fun events and festivals taking place geared towards kids. The museums often have interesting workshops planned, and theatres offer a programme specially tailored for children. Go to **www.visitdublin.com** for a list of what's happening for children in Dublin.

and feeding times hold their attention.

Viking Splash Tours
St Stephen's Green North (start point); tel: 01 707 6000; www.vikingsplash.ie; Mar–Nov daily, call or check website for times; admission charge; bus: 92, 118, 746; map p.137 C2

While adults also enjoy the history behind this tour over land and water, kids just enjoy playing out the role of a Viking warrior on board this unique form of transport that takes the guise of a Viking ship.
SEE ALSO WALKS, BUS TOURS AND BOAT TRIPS, P.127

OUTDOORS
Dublin Zoo
Phoenix Park; tel: 01 474 8900; www.dublinzoo.ie; Mar–Sept daily 9.30am–6pm, Nov–Feb daily 9.30am–dusk; admission charge; bus: 10, 25, 26; Luas: Heuston Station then shuttle bus daily 7am–6pm (starts 10am Sat and Sun), departs on the hour every hour; map p.130 A3

Ireland's largest zoo, set in 12 hectares (30 acres), houses over 235 species of animals and tropical birds and is all about fun, learning and conservation. The easily navigated areas allow visitors to spot Asian elephants in the **Rainforest**, discover zebra on the **Plains of Africa**, hunt lions in the **World of Cats** or be amused by the monkeys at the **World of Primates**. Children love the train that trundles around the zoo, and the keeper talks

Churches

The oldest medieval church in Dublin is
Christ Church Cathedral, commissioned
in 1172, and the oldest parish church is St
Audoen's (c.1190), which can be found by the
only remaining city gate, St Audoen's Arch,
which itself dates to 1215. There were wooden
churches before this date, but none have
survived. After the desecration caused by the
Reformation, many of the city's churches fell
into disrepair, but were later restored with the
aid of wealthy Victorian Dubliners. The
affluent Georgians preferred to build their
churches in the smarter districts.

SOUTH OF THE LIFFEY, WEST

Christ Church Cathedral

Christchurch Place; tel: 01 677
8099; www.cccdub.ie;
June–Aug Mon–Fri 9.45am–
6.15pm, Sat 9.45am–4.15pm,
Sun 12.30pm–2.30pm,
4.30pm–6.15pm, June–mid-
July Wed–Thur until 4.15pm,
Sept–May Mon–Sat 9.45–
4.15pm, Sun 12.30pm–2.30pm;

While Dublin's two Protestant
cathedrals take pride of place,
St Mary's Pro-Cathedral (85
Marlborough Street; tel: 01
8745441; www.procathedral.ie;
Mon–Fri 7.30am–6.45pm, Sat
7.30am–7.15pm, Sun 9am–
1.45pm and 5.30pm–7.45pm;
free; bus: 142; map p.132 C2),
representative of a predominantly Catholic country, is hidden
away off the beaten track behind
O'Connell Street, reflecting the
political stance when it was built
in 1825. The word 'Pro' indicates
it is an acting cathedral and thus
has never been given the true
status afforded to the other two.
Built in the neoclassical Doric
style, it is well known for its
excellent Palestrina Choir.

admission charge; bus: 50,
56a, 123; map p.136 A4
The church that first stood
on this site over 1,000 years
ago was made of wood,
founded by Sitric Silken-
beard, the first Christian
king of the Dublin Norse-
men. The Normans demol-
ished the church, and a
stone version was commis-
sioned in 1180. Passing into
Protestant hands after the
Reformation, the cathedral
has remained dedicated to
the Church of Ireland. Highlights include the crypt and
the exhibition **Treasures of
Christ Church**, and the
12th-century transept.

St Patrick's Cathedral

St Patrick's Street; tel: 01 453
9472; www.stpatrickscathe
dral.ie; daily 9am–5.30pm
(Nov–Feb Sat until 5pm, Sun
until 3pm); admission charge;
bus: 50, 56a, 77; map p.136 A2
St Patrick's Cathedral
enjoys a more open
position than Christ Church,
set in a large park a short
walk from the city centre.
Founded as a church in
1192, it was built in the

early English Gothic style
and finally completed in
1284. It too was dedicated
to the Church of Ireland and
heavily restored in the 19th
century from funds donated
by the Guinness family.
Jonathan Swift, famous for
his book *Gulliver's Travels*,
was Dean here from 1713
until his death in 1745. Regular tours give an insight
into the history of the building, which has the largest
church organ in Ireland.

Whitefriar Street Carmelite Church

56 Aungier Street; tel: 01 475
8821; Mon–Fri 7.45am–6pm,

Left: the impressive Christ Church Cathedral.

Music has played an important part in the history of Dublin's churches, and concerts are a regular feature of church life today. *See also Music, p.90.*

The position of this church in the heart of the affluent Georgian district of the city saw it endowed with money from influential residents. The 1707 church had an imposing neo-Romanesque facade added in 1868. It has some excellent examples of stained glass dating from the mid-19th century.

Tue until 9.15pm, Sat–Sun 7.45am–7.30pm; free; bus: 16a, 19a, 83; map p.136 B3
Highlights of this 1825 church administered by the Carmelite order are the Shrine of Our Lady of Dublin, the Well of St Albert of Sicily and the shrine containing the remains of St Valentine, making it a pilgrimage church for lovers.

ST. STEPHEN'S GREEN AND AROUND
University Church
87a St Stephen's Green; tel: 01 478 1606; www.university church.ie; Mon–Sat 9am–5.30pm, Sun 10am–1pm,

Left and below: at the historic St Patrick's Cathedral.

5am–6pm; free; bus: 14a, 15a, 128; map p.136 C2
Nestled between Nos. 86 and 87, this remarkable church was built on the commission by Cardinal John Henry Newman. The neo-Byzantine interior is beautiful, and it is a popular venue for weddings.

GEORGIAN DISTRICT AND MUSEUMS
St Ann's
Dawson Street; tel: 01 676 7727; Mon–Fri 10am–4pm, Sun services; free; bus: 10a, 128, 746; map p.137 C3

NORTH OF THE LIFFEY, WEST
St Michan's
Church Street; tel: 01 872 4154; Mar–Oct Mon–Fri 10am–12.45pm, 2–4.30pm, Sat 10am–12.45pm, Nov–Feb 12.30pm–3.30pm, Sat 10am–12.45pm, Sun services all year; admission charge; bus: 66, 83; Luas: Four Courts, Smithfield; map p.131 E1
Rather drab from the outside, St Michan's holds a dark secret within its vaults. Take a guided tour to see the extraordinarily well-preserved mummified bodies, complete with hair and skin.

43

DART Excursions

Dublin's scenic light-railway service, the DART (Dublin Area Rapid Transit), was created in 1984 but has undergone many modifications over the years. An attraction in its own right, visitors can enjoy an inexpensive and fun day out on the DART. There are stunning views as the carriages trundle their way from Malahide in the north to Greystones in the south. You can stay on board and soak up the view, or alternatively, hop off at the individual coastal settlements' stations scattered along the track. Note that it's best to avoid the rush hour, as the carriages can get extremely crowded. *See also Transport, p.123.*

BRAY

From what was a refined Victorian resort in the 1830s, the lively seaside town of Bray embraces hordes of families during the holiday season. Amusements and attractions along the esplanade keep the children entertained when they are not playing on the safe sand and shingle beach that stretches for 1.5km (1 mile).

The National Sealife Centre

tel: 01 286 6939; www.sealifeeurope.com; Mar–Oct daily 10am–5pm, Nov–Feb Mon–Fri 11am–4pm, Sat–Sun 10am–5pm; admission charge

This sealife centre on the seafront gives a conservation-conscious insight into life under the sea, where you will encounter strange inhabitants that lurk there. Adults are catered for, too, with golf, sailing and fishing on the doorstep, or a wander from Bray Harbour to Bray Head is a popular way to while away an hour or two.

DALKEY

South of Dublin, the pretty village centre of Dalkey is just a short stroll from the DART station. Once called the 'Town of Seven Castles', only two of these fortified mansions remain facing each other across the main street. One of these, **Goat Castle**, gives access to the Heritage Centre. In summer a boat ferries visitors over to **Dalkey Island**, which is mostly turned over to a bird reserve.

Some excellent pubs and restaurants make a visit to Dalkey even more enjoyable; try the **Guinea Pig**, which has been serv-

The streets of Dublin are no longer blessed with many good markets, hence many bargain-hunters jump on the DART and flock to Blackrock for one of Dublin's best-run and most successful weekend markets (Sat 11am–5.30pm, Sun noon–5.30pm). Around 50 stalls are set up indoors and out, which tout a unique mix of wares ranging from clothes, bric-a-brac and fine art to crafts, antiques and books.

Left: resting in a picturesque Wicklow Mountains town.

GREYSTONES

At the south end of the DART line 28km (18 miles) out of Dublin, Greystones provides a gateway to the magnificent Wicklow Mountains and the famous Sugarloaf Mountain, which looms over the town to the west. The name is derived from a long, wide outcrop of grey rocks that stretch between the town's two beaches. The stony North Beach starts at the harbour and is overlooked by the southern cliffs of Bray Head.

South Beach is a long, broad sandy stretch that has been awarded the coveted Blue Flag and consequently receives many visitors in the summer months. Despite growing into a thriving town over the past 10 years, Greystones has retained its former village atmosphere. There is an abundance of cafés and

ing some of the best fish dishes in the area since 1957. Dalkey's other claim to fame is its literary connections with George Bernard Shaw, who lived in Dalkey, and James Joyce, who set chapter two of *Ulysses* here.

SEE ALSO LITERATURE, P.76

Heritage Centre

Castle Street; tel: 01 285 8366; www.dalkeycastle.com; Mon–Fri 9.30am–5pm; Sat–Sun 11am–5pm; admission charge
This excellent resource in Goat Castle holds reconstructions of Dalkey when it was an important port in its own right; there are splendid views of the sea and mountains from the battlements.

DÚN LAOGHAIRE

At the weekend, many city folk take the 15-minute journey on the DART south to Dublin's thriving ferry port to escape the

Left: Dún Laoghaire's seafront.

city bustle. Consider a stroll on the pier, where the occasional concert is staged on the bandstand, or a bracing walk along the elegant Victorian seafront to Sandycove (see p.47) for perfect solitude. There are plenty of nice spots to eat and drink while watching the car ferries ply across the water.

Below: in the Wicklow Mountains.

restaurants to choose from, a charming harbour and great opportunities for peaceful walks.

HOWTH

This traditional fishing village, which spreads out over a bulbous promontory to the north of Dublin, these days attracts as many yachts to its marina as fishing boats. A short, steep walk down from the DART station leads through the pretty town to waterside bars and restaurants. Many visitors head for **Howth Castle** and the **National Transport Museum**; the castle is closed to the public, but the gardens are worth visiting in May and June, when they are ablaze with colourful rhododendrons.

For dramatic views take the cliff-top walk that snakes around Howth Head.

National Transport Museum

Heritage Depot, Howth Demesne; tel: 01 832 0427; www.nationaltransportmu seum.org; Sept–May Sat–Sun 2pm–5pm, June–Aug Mon–Sat 10pm–5pm; admission charge
This museum represents over 120 years of transport history. Some 60 vehicles are on display, covering five sections devoted to Passenger, Commercial, Fire and Emergency, Military and Utility modes of transport.

KILLINEY

The affluent seaside suburb of Killiney, affectionately known as 'Dublin's Riviera', has a certain appeal that attracts the rich and famous to set up home here. Unfortunately, the price of property makes Killiney a place that the majority can only afford to visit. A curving sandy beach with stunning gorse-covered hills as a backdrop and a walk along the Vico Road, from where there are some of the most breathtaking views in and around Dublin, make it easy to understand why. In summer, fishermen run boats trips from **Coliemore Harbour** to nearby Dalkey Island (see p.44), a piece of land captured by the Vikings, later occupied by Christian communities and now a bird sanctuary.

MALAHIDE

As attractive as this seaside town is, with its newly developed marina and chic shops, most visitors disembark the train and take the 10-minute walk to **Malahide Castle**.

Below: boats lined up in Howth's marina.

Right: the medieval Malahide Castle.

Left: you can enjoy a spot of fishing in Howth.

Malahide Castle

Tel: 01 846 2184; www.malahidecastle.com; daily 10am–5pm; admission charge

Standing in beautiful parkland, the core of the castle is a medieval tower adjoining a banquet hall that is adorned with Talbot family portraits; the family lived here for nearly 800 years from 1188 until 1973.

SANDYCOVE

Mainly an affluent commuter suburb, Sandycove is known for its long seaside promenade that eventually links up with Dun Laoghaire, the next stop on the DART. It is also famous for its **Martello Tower**, standing on a rocky point, originally built during the Napoleonic Wars to withstand invasion. Considering writer James Joyce

Birdwatching enthusiasts might want to get off for a few minutes at Booterstown, famed for its designated bird sanctuary. The marshlands beside the track are a protected feeding and nesting area for many interesting species, which are identified on a board erected on the station platform.

chose the tower as the setting for the first chapter of his masterpiece *Ulysses*, it is a fitting tribute that it now holds the **James Joyce Museum**, which is devoted to his life.

James Joyce Museum

Martello Tower; tel: 01 280 9265; Apr–Sept Tue–Sat 10am–5pm, Sun 2pm–6pm; admission charge

Joyce memorabilia displayed include letters, photographs, first and rare editions and personal items such as his guitar.

SEE ALSO LITERATURE, P.76

Fry Model Railway Museum

Malahide Castle; Apr–Sept Tue–Sat 10am–5pm, Sun 1–5pm; admission charge

Situated in a separate building in Malahide Castle's grounds is the one of the world's largest collections of model railways, including an exhibit of Dublin landmarks in miniature.

Environment

Environmental issues are certainly to the fore in Dublin, but it is a slow process to reduce emissions. Sustainability is being promoted by Dublin City Council, which is encouraging the public, businesses and hoteliers to 'go green'. Developments in public transport have improved things, especially the DART and the economical Luas. Modern buildings in the developing Docklands area are being built with strong green credentials and organic farmers' markets are booming, while local produce is a must for many restaurants. Waterways are being cleaned up, and the city benefits from excellent parks and gardens.

PUBLIC TRANSPORT

Extensions to both the DART (Dublin Area Rapid Transit) and the state-of-the-art Luas light-rail tram system will increase the numbers of commuters leaving their cars at home when coming to work in Dublin. Both methods of transport are energy-efficient and produce little pollution. Traffic in Dublin has been an ongoing problem, and it is hoped that the building of the Port Tunnel will ease congestion. A new underground metro planned for north Dublin will hopefully improve the situation further.

SEE ALSO TRANSPORT, P.123

ECOCABS AND CYCLING

When the concept of rickshaws was first introduced to Dublin in 1996 it proved a bit of a shock for tourists and visitors alike. Those on a night out in Temple Bar began to use them to

go from pub to pub, or to the clubs. Subsequently various companies have run rickshaw rides, but the novelty wore off, and with a drop in tourists after 9/11 the companies ceased.

Currently environmentally friendly coloured ecocabs (www.ecocabs.ie), which run from 1 April to 31 December from 10am–7pm, can be seen around the city. These are free, with revenue generated by the advertising covering the cab paying for the riders. There are eight designated pick-up points, and the service works with a 2km (1¼-mile) radius of O'Connell Bridge. Enquire at the tourist office for more information. It's a great way to cross the city without polluting it.

The Dublin Cycling Campaign has been working since the early 1990s to encourage cycling in the city and to increase

Left: the Luas light-rail network is environmentally conscious.

Left: Dublin is a great city to cycle in.

are located in the suburbs, at the Liffey Valley Shopping Centre and Monkstown, and the Dublin Food Co-op in the suburb of Newmarket is dedicated to produce produced by environmentally friendly means. Restaurateurs and top chefs are increasingly choosing to use local, fresh ingredients. Cultivate *(see below)* sells eco-friendly products. SEE ALSO FOOD AND DRINK, P.60

ENVIRONMENTAL ORGANISATIONS

Cultivate – Sustainable Living Centre
15–19 Essex Street West, Temple Bar; tel: 01 674 5773; www.cultivate.ie; bus: 50, 78a, 66a; map p.136 A4
Cultivate is a resource and information centre dedicated to sustainability and to providing Dubliners with advice on climate change and energy issues. As well as hosting workshops, talks and events, it runs a seriously good eco-shop. All organic, environmentally friendly and fair-trade needs are addressed here, plus a courtyard garden and nursery for buying plants.

Dublin City Council
Civic Offices, Wood Quay; tel: 01 676 7727; www.dublin.ie; bus: 66a, 66b, 78a; map p.132 C2
Check out the excellent website on all environmental issues in the city. The Environmental Focus Group was formed in 2002 to promote all aspects of sustaining a 'greener Dublin'.

Dublin has a rich and varied biodiversity. The city maintains many habitats and ecosystems within the parks, nature reserves, canals, gardens and beaches, inhabited by a rich variety of flora and fauna. Of the 33 species of Irish mammals, 28 are found within a 20-km (12½-mile) radius of central Dublin. For more exotic wildlife, visit Dublin Zoo in Phoenix Park, an organisation dedicated to the research and conservation of endangered species. *See also Children, p.41.*

Above: organic produce at Temple Bar Food Market.

public awareness of cyclists. Dublin City Council is eager to promote cycling and is at present preparing cycle-lane maps of the city.

Phoenix Park Bike Hire (www.phoenixparkbike hire.com) rent out bikes at the Parkgate entrance to Phoenix Park, with the opportunity of cycling around the city. All cyclists should be aware of the dangers of traffic. SEE ALSO PARKS AND GARDENS, P.96

GREEN SHOPPING

There is an active campaign to promote local produce and a green approach to shopping in Dublin, which includes some excellent organic and farmers' markets in the city. A new farmers' market was launched in May 2009 in the colonnades of the Bank of Ireland, while the Temple Bar Food Market, held on Saturdays, is a food paradise of local produce. Other farmers' markets

Essentials

In a city where the residents have a reputation as being some of the friendliest in the world, you shouldn't have much trouble finding out what you need to know. Just stop on the street, produce a map, look bemused, and a member of the public will soon be at your side offering helpful advice. Dubliners are proud of their compact city, which caters well for visitors and is reasonably free of crime. Do not be fooled by the laid-back atmosphere compared to other Western European cities: the standard of service is just as high these days, and it's generally delivered with a smile.

CLIMATE
The weather can be unpredictable, so plan for sun, wind and rain all in one day. Dublin has less rain than the rest of Ireland, but it can still be pretty soggy year-round. Spring is generally mild, with a mix of sunshine and showers. June to August is the warmest time, but excessive heat is rare, and in July there are often showers. There can be heavy rain in autumn, although it is generally mild, with the odd bright day here and there. Winter is usually wet rather than cold, and conditions are rarely severe.

CRIME AND SAFETY
Don't be unduly perturbed if a stranger strikes up a conversation, as Dubliners are very friendly, but at the same time use your instincts. Dublin is still relatively safe, but levels of street crime have risen in recent years, and pickpockets and bag-snatchers are fairly prevalent, so keep a watchful eye on your valuables. Avoid certain areas after dark: Fitzwilliam and Merrion squares are prime prostitution spots, and Phoenix Park is a less than desirable place to be after dark. When travelling on the bus at night, exercise caution and sit downstairs close to the driver. Garda (police) patrol the streets, and are very approachable if you are concerned.

DISABLED TRAVELLERS
Things are steadily improving in Dublin for people with disabilities. All new Dublin buses have incorporated ramps, wider gangways and priority spaces, and some older buses have been adapted. This is limited to certain routes, so it's best to check with **Dublin Bus** (see p.123) before travelling. The Luas is fully equipped for mobility and sensory impairments, but the DART is more restricted. Several attractions now have ramps and lifts, as do restaurants and hotels.

Emergency Contacts
For police, fire and ambulance dial 999 or 112.
The **Irish Tourist Assistance Service** (ITAS; Garda Headquarters; Harcourt Street; tel: 01-478 5295) offers support and practical assistance to tourists who are victims of crime while in Ireland. This service is free, but the ITAS suggest the incident be reported to the nearest police station first and they will then contact the ITAS.

Below: mounted Garda patrolling the streets.

Left: Dublin's Tourist Information Office.

need to obtain this card before leaving home.

HOSPITALS AND DENTISTS

Anne's Lane Dental Centre
2 St Anne's Lane; tel: 01 671 8581; www.anneslanedental centre.com; bus: 10a, 128, 746; map p.136 B3
Just off Grafton Street, the centre will provide emergency treatment on a daily basis.

Beaumont Hospital
Beaumont Road; tel: 01 809 3000; www.beaumont.ie; bus: 27b, 41a/b, 104
Located on the north side of the city, this is one of the largest general hospitals in the Dublin area and offers an accident and emergency department.

St James's Hospital
James Street, Kilmainham; tel: 01 410 3000; www.stjames.ie; bus: 51b/c, 78a, 123; map p.134 B2
One of the stops on the Luas, St James's provides the community with a comprehensive accident and emergency department.

St Vincent's Hospital
Elm Park; tel: 01 221 4000; www.stvincents.ie; bus: 2, 7, 8
A major teaching hospital affiliated with University College Dublin, southeast of Ballsbridge, which offers 24-hour accident and emergency service.

INTERNET
Various places provide Wifi internet access throughout the city, including book-shops, cafés, hotels and

Irish Wheelchair Association
Blackheath Drive, Clontarf; tel: 01 818 6400; www.iwa.ie
This organisation can provide more detailed information on accessibility and contacts for wheelchair hire.

ELECTRICITY
The standard electricity power supply is 220–240v, 50-cycle AC voltage, and sockets are the same as the UK, with three square pins. Most hotels have a 110v outlet for shavers. Plug adaptors are available from electrical suppliers around the city and at the airport.

EMBASSIES AND CONSULATES
Australian Embassy:
Fitzwilliam House, Wilton Place; tel: 01 664 5300; www.ireland.embassy.gov.au
British Embassy:
29 Merrion Road, Ballsbridge; tel: 01 205 3700; www.britishembassy.ie
New Zealand Consulate:
37 Leeson Park; tel: 01 660

Above: only guide dogs allowed here.

4233; www.nzembassy.com
United States Embassy:
42 Elgin Road, Ballsbridge; tel: 01 668 8777; www.dublin.usembassy.gov

HEALTH AND MEDICAL CARE
Check your travel insurance coverage before leaving to make sure it's comprehensive enough. EU nationals or those with whom Ireland has a reciprocal agreement receive free or reduced-cost medical treatment if they carry an **EHIC** (European Health Insurance Card). You will

Left: a handily prominent post box.

bureaux de change at the airport, tourist office and all banks, while larger post offices have currency exchange facilities too. Major hotels, restaurants and shops accept all major credit cards, although some smaller businesses may not.

ATMS are found all over the city and can be accessed by foreign debit or credit cards carrying the Visa, MasterCard, Cirrus or Plus logo.

PHARMACIES

Prescription and non-prescription drugs are available at the many pharmacies scattered around the city, and pharmacists are willing to offer advice on minor ailments. When closed, most pharmacists display details of the nearest one that will be open.

hostels. Cyber cafés come and go all the time but the below outlet manages to see off all the competition.

Global Internet Café

8 Lower O'Connell Street; tel: 01 878 0295; www.global cafe.ie; Mon–Fri 8am–11pm, Sat 9am–11pm, Sun 10am– 11pm; map p.132 C2
High-quality equipment and knowledgeable staff are the key to their success, and they also claim to have the fastest internet connection in Dublin.

MEDIA

The main daily broadsheets are the *Irish Times* and *Irish Independent*. The *Evening Herald*, which hits the shelves Monday to Friday at midday, is useful for cinema listings and events.

Most English tabloids are available, but in a revamped format to suit the Irish market.

For further event listings, pick up a copy of the *Event Guide*, a free weekly newspaper full of useful listings. *InDublin* magazine, available from newsagents, is a directory covering movies, music, theatre and lots more.

MONEY MATTERS

The euro (€) is the Republic of Ireland's currency unit, which is divided into 100 cents. Euro notes come in denominations of 5, 10, 20, 50, 100, 200 and 500; coins are 1, 2, 5, 10, 20 and 50 cents, as well as €1 and €2. Check www.xe.com for current exchange rates. There are

O'Connell's

55 Lower O'Connell Street; tel: 01 873 0427; Mon–Sat 8am–10pm, Sun 10am–10pm; bus: 10a, 14a, 46a; map p.132 C2
Late services in a handy location.

POSTAL SERVICES

The Irish postal service is called **An Post**. Post offices are generally open Mon–Fri 9am–5.30pm and some Sat 9am–1pm; note that many branches close for lunch.

Stamps are available from post offices, newsstands, hotels and shops, and from coin-operated machines outside post

Right: a police car speeds through the streets.

offices and in some shopping centres.

General Post Office
O'Connell Street; tel: 01 705 8833; www.anpost.ie; Mon–Sat 8am–8pm; bus: 10a, 14a, 46a; map p.132 C2
The city's main post office has the longest opening hours.

TELEPHONES
Most public telephones take coins or phonecards (available in post offices and newsagents); some take credit cards. When dialling Ireland from outside the city, use the area code 01. To dial an Ireland number from a public phone inside the city, you do not need to use the code, just dial the seven-digit number.

If you are calling a local number from your mobile phone it will be necessary to dial 00353 (for Ireland) followed by the code for Dublin (01), because you are still operating through your home service provider. Call 11850 for operator directory

enquires; numbers preceded with 1800 are toll-free.

TOURIST INFORMATION
Main Tourist
Information Office
St Andrew's Church, Suffolk Street; tel: 01 605 7700; www.visitdublin.com; Mon–Sat 9am–5.30pm, Sun 10.30am–3pm, July–Aug 9am–7pm, longer hours in summer; bus: 10a, 13a, 15a; map p.136 C4
There are four further walk-in centres at 14 Upper O'Connell Street, Dublin Airport, Dun Laoghaire Harbour, The Square and Tallaght.

VISAS
Entry requirements are subject to change and differ depending on nationality. It is advisable to check well in advance of your travel dates with the embassy or consulate in your home country, or go to their website. Visitors from the UK do not require a passport to enter Dublin, but it is best to carry one as photo ID is required to prove UK nationality.

The loss of a passport or anything valuable should be reported to the police immediately, who will then issue a reference number to validate any insurance claim. Contact the **Garda Carriage Office** located in Dublin Castle (tel: 01 666 9857) for anything left behind in a taxi. There are lost property offices at Connolly Station (tel: 01 703 2359) and Dublin Bus (tel: 01 703 1321).

WEBSITES
www.discoverireland.com
All you need to know about Ireland from the Irish Tourist Board.

www.dublinevents.com
A comprehensive guide to things to do, places to go, where to stay and eat, and other useful information.

www.eventguide.ie
The online version of the *Event Guide* about forthcoming events in the city.

www.visitdublin.com
Dublin's comprehensive official tourist site is kept up to date.

Festivals and Events

The fun-loving Irish relish the chance to dress up and frolic in the streets – and you will be hard-pushed to not join in the fun. With an exhaustive line-up of vibrant festivals and events, the chances are there will be something going on whenever you are in Dublin, whether it be a music festival, major sporting event or religious festival. Check if your visit coincides with a key date, as hotels get booked up very quickly at these times. Major events are listed below; for specialised events see *Gay and Lesbian, p.63*.

JAN–FEB
Jameson Dublin International Film Festival
12–22 Feb; various venues; www.jdiff.com
Ten-day festival devoted to Irish and international cinema. Besides the chance to catch some great movies, there are several non-screening events to get involved in. The festival is becoming increasingly popular, so it's best to book tickets in advance.

MAR–APR
St Patrick's Day Festival
Early Mar; various venues; www.stpatricksfestival.ie
The most popular annual festival in Dublin always commences the week leading up to St Patrick's Day. Once a humdrum religious event with a rather gloomy procession, today this festival has grown into an extravaganza of street performers, fireworks and lots of drinking, plus a full calendar of concerts and exhibitions all building up to a huge parade on the last day. Visitors come from afar to the join in the jollity.

MAY–JUNE
Dublin Dance Festival
Early May; various venues; www.dublindancefestival.ie
A two-week festival dedicated to promoting contemporary dance in Ireland. Award-winning dancers from around the world take to the stage to give performances that draw on their very different dance styles.

Dublin City Soul Festival
Mid-May; various venues; www.dublincitysoulfestival.ie
Fairly new to the Dublin festival scene, this funky four-day festival is a cele-

Left: several events in Dublin involve a few pints.

Left: on parade at the St Patrick's Day Festival.

calendar, the world's best show horses and best international show jumpers descend on Dublin for Ireland's equestrian event of the year.

SEPT–OCT

Ulster Bank Dublin Theatre Festival

Late Sept–early Oct; various venues; www.dublintheatrefestival.com

Founded in 1957, this is Europe's oldest event of its kind and one of Dublin's biggest annual festivals. Over a two-week period it showcases contemporary Irish drama, and most leading names from the drama scene take part.

Adidas Dublin Marathon

Oct; start Fitzwilliam Square, finish Merrion Square West; www.dublinmarathon.ie

Thousands of enthusiastic runners gather on the last Monday in October to compete in the annual Dublin marathon through the spectator-lined streets.

Below: a portrait of the artist: celebrating Bloomsday.

When in Dublin, if you catch sight of some 400 men and women plunging into the murky River Liffey on a chilly September day, don't be concerned: there is a reasonable explanation. They are taking part in the annual Liffey Swim, an extraordinary tradition that has survived for over 85 years. The race is over an exhausting 1,800m/yds past many bemused ducks and historical landmarks, but the swimmers are too intent on winning to appreciate the sights.

bration of soul music. The Soul Picnic in Merrion Square is particularly good fun – local and international artists give performances in the park, admission is free, and don't forget your blanket.

Docklands Maritime Festival

May/June; Docklands; www.dublindocklands.ie

A growing event where a fleet of tall ships takes centre stage while colourful street performers on the quayside create a carnival atmosphere. The festival also features an outdoor market with over 80 stalls selling gourmet delights and Irish crafts.

Bloomsday Festival

Around 16 June; various venues; www.jamesjoyce.ie

This annual event is a tribute to 16 June, the day on which James Joyce set his novel *Ulysses*. The festival runs for five days, and Joycean fans celebrate the great author's life through dressing up and walks that follow in the footsteps of Leopold Bloom (Joyce's central character), plus there are readings, performances, film screenings and special events for children, which all help to set the scene in Dublin around 1904.

JULY–AUG

Failte Ireland Dublin Horse Show

Early Aug; RDS Grounds; www.dublinhorseshow.com

A highlight on the summer

Film

Dublin's film industry may not rank alongside Hollywood, but it has been responsible for some glorious moments on the silver screen. The Irish are known for telling a tale, and international film producers are drawn to this city that offers many natural backdrops for their work. Dubliners also like to catch a movie; the city has one of the highest per capita cinema attendances in Europe. In addition, the cultural quarter of Temple Bar has worked hard to promote aspiring filmmakers and preserve film culture at some of its venues. A highlight of the year is the Jameson International Film Festival *(see Festivals and Events, p.54)*.

FAMOUS DUBLINERS

Dublin has spawned many great actors. Born in the Dublin suburb of Castlenock, the infamous **Colin Farrell** was a former footballer with Shamrock Rovers FC. He has worked on many box office successes, including *Intermission* (2003), which was actually filmed in Dublin.

Brenda Fricker successfully moved from her television role in the BBC's *Casualty* to the big screen when she won an Oscar for her role in *My Left Foot*.

Others major actors include **Michael Gambon**, **Richard Todd**, **Sinéad Cusack** and **Jonathan Rhys Meyers**, whose body of work ranges from a Woody Allen film, *Match Point*, to the television series *The Tudors*. Dubliner **Jim Sheridan** has made his name as director of some of the best Irish-themed films, such as *My Left Foot* and *In the Name of the Father*. Another Dubliner emerging as a new talent is director **Damien O'Donnell**, whose debut movie was the BAFTA nominated *East is East* (1999).

ON LOCATION

Some of the most important Irish films have been made on location in Dublin. Trinity College took a starring role in *Educating Rita* (1983), and *My Left Foot* (1989) portrayed the grimmer side of north Dublin while telling the life story of the Irish writer Christy Brown, who had cerebral palsy.

Parts of *The Italian Job* were filmed in Kilmainham Gaol *(see Museums and Galleries, p.79)*, while the epic tale of *Michael Collins* (1996) and the Irish struggle for independence was filmed at several locations around the city.

The 2003 film *Veronica Guerin* was a true-life recounting of the titular Irish crime reporter who was murdered for her drug-world investigations.

Central Dublin has a few cinemas, but it's the out-of-town multiplexes that attract serious numbers; they are mostly easily accessible by public transport. The UCI group has huge multiplexes in Tallaght, Blanchardstown and Coolock. **Vue** (tel: 01 605 5700), at the Liffey Valley Shopping Centre in Clondalkin, offers the ultimate cinema experience, featuring some of the largest screens in Europe (one claimed to be as big as a tennis court).

A JERRY BRUCKHEIMER PRODUCTION A FILM BY JOEL SCHUMACHER

VERONICA GUERIN

Left: Irish actors Brendan Gleeson and Colin Farrell in the 2008 hit film, *In Bruges.*

arthouse, foreign and documentary films screened here.

Lighthouse Cinema

Market Square, Smithfield; tel: 01 879 7601; www.lighthouse cinema.ie; bus: 66, 83; Luas: Smithfield; map p.135 C3

This four-screen, 600-seat cultural cinema presents a diverse programme of the best Irish, independent, foreign-language, arthouse and classic cinema.

MAINSTREAM CINEMAS
Cineworld

Parnell Street; tel: 01 872 8444; www.cineworld.ie; bus: 37, 39a, 70a; Luas: Jervis; map p.132 A2

The largest cinema in the city centre has 17 screens showing all the latest blockbusters. Other entertainment includes simulated rides and computer games, and there are bars, restaurants and fast-food outlets.

It starred Cate Blanchett and was also shot on location in Dublin.

ARTHOUSE CINEMAS
Irish Film Institute

6 Eustace Street, Temple Bar; tel: 01 679 5744; www.irish film.ie; bus: 50, 66a, 66b; map p.136 A1

A weekly membership gives you and three guests the opportunity to appreciate the selection of

Left: Cate Blanchett in the poster for *Veronica Guerin.*

Savoy Cinema

17 Upper O'Connell Street; tel: 0818 776 776; www.omniplex.ie; bus: 14a, 16a, 746; map p.132 C2

Dublin's oldest remaining cinema has had many of its 1920s features recreated after major refurbishment – chandeliers, an Italian marble foyer, grand staircases and walnut panelled walls. Modern concessions include five wide screens.

Screen

D'Olier Street; tel: 0818 300 301; www.omniplex.ie; bus: 1, 2, 50; DART: Tara Street; map p.133 C1

An old favourite with three screens, renowned for showing films that you might not come across at other cinemas.

Below: a statue of the real-life Veronica Guerin.

Food and Drink

The diverse range of cuisine and restaurants on offer make eating out in Dublin generally a similar experience to in any other cosmopolitan city in Europe *(see Restaurants, p.100)*. However, visitors may still wonder what the locals eat and whether there is such a thing as an Irish cuisine. The answer to this question is that there certainly is, and although traditional dishes may have been given a modern twist, there is some excellent Irish cooking demonstrated at many establishments, using top-quality local produce. Be sure to seek out one of these eateries and sample good homely Irish cooking.

HISTORY OF IRISH FOOD AND THE POTATO FAMINE

Owing to a temperate climate, the growing of staple crops, such as oats, barley and some vegetables, has always been at the heart of the basic Irish diet, along with venison, beef and pork when it was available. With the introduction of the potato in the 16th century a new staple was

added; it became one of the most important and infamous foods in Ireland. It fed those on a subsistence diet as well as the pigs that most of the poor kept. As a result, people were extremely vulnerable in times of failing potato harvests. As the population grew these poor harvests had a devastating effect, with the first serious recorded famine in 1739, but it was the famines between 1845 and 1849, known as the Great Famine, that decimated the population. Nearly 1 million people died, over 2 million emigrated and 3 million were left destitute.

TRADITIONAL IRISH FOODS

Irish cooking produces some wonderfully rich flavours, and although it is known for heavy, hearty concoctions originally intended for farmers and fishermen, the dishes have

been modernised and refined for a less active society.

Particular favourites include **Dublin coddle**, a type of sausage or shellfish stew; **Irish stew**, cooked using lamb, beef or mutton, with the flavour further enhanced by the addition of stout; **colcannon**, made of mashed potatoes and cabbage, once a cheap staple food – now refined with Irish bacon, cream and garlic; **champ**, a similar dish using potatoes and scallions (spring onions); the **boxty**, a potato pancake with a savoury filling; and **Irish soda bread**, a bread made using baking soda rather than yeast.

IRISH DRINKS

GUINNESS

No trip to Dublin would be complete without a pint of the 'black stuff' or at least a visit to the **Guinness Storehouse** *(see also*

Left: a hearty Irish stew.

Right: delectable soda bread.

Left: goodies from the Avoca shop *(see p.60)*.

apart from other whiskeys owing to the Irish practice of triple distillation, which is still used in production today. You can learn all about the process and a try a sample at the **Old Jameson Distillery** in Smithfield.

SEE ALSO MUSEUMS AND GALLERIES, P.86

IRISH COFFEE

Known as *Caife Gaelach*, and invented in County Limerick in the 1940s, this after-dinner cocktail of hot coffee, Irish whiskey and optional sugar is drunk through a head of cream. The invention was a simple response by chef Joseph Sheridan to the needs of recently arrived American passengers in the restaurant at Foynes Airport. Seeing that they were chilled by the cool Irish night he added whiskey to their coffee and the Irish coffee was born.

Bars and Cafés, p.32) to learn about the impact this drink and the family brewery has had on the city. In fact the largest consumer of Guinness today is Nigeria, overtaking Ireland in sales in 2007. Although the company makes no claims of the health advantages of the drink these days, the 'Guinness is Good for You' advertising campaign, which began in the 1920s, is still used overseas.

WHISKEY

It is believed that Irish missionary monks brought the art of distilling whiskey to Europe as early as the 12th century. This drink, *uisce beatha* or 'water of life', is set

Is it whiskey or whisky? Visitors to Ireland may wonder about this difference in spelling (although those from the US will feel at home). Originally all whisky was spelt without the extra 'e', but the story goes that towards the end of the 19th century the reputation of Scottish whisky was poor, with some distilleries producing cheaper versions. At this time the Irish and American distilleries adopted the extra 'e' to distinguish their high-quality product, and until this day they are still the only two countries to spell the 'amber nectar' this way.

Left: fresh fruit and vegetables at the Temple Bar Food Market.

Temple Bar Food Market
Meeting House Square, Temple Bar; tel: 01 677 2255; www.templebar.ie; Sat 10am–4.30pm; bus: 50, 66a, 66b; map p.136 A1
This outdoor market in the heart of the Temple Bar is a foodies' paradise; a delicious blend of colours, smells and tastes. Here you will find a market dedicated to locally sourced, seasonal food with a few exotic culinary delights to tickle your taste buds further. Plenty of gorgeous goodies to take home or eat on site, including Irish cheeses, jams, pastries, fruits and vegetables. This is one not to be missed.

FOOD MARKETS
Epicurean Food Hall
Liffey Street Lower; Mon–Wed 9am–7pm, Thur–Fri 9am–8.30pm, Sat 9am–6.30pm; bus: 10a, 14a, 46a, Luas: Jervis; map p.132 B1
Located on the corner of Liffey Street and Middle Abbey Street, this hall is made up of a collection of small units and stalls and a common seating area. There is a good range of gourmet foods, both cooked and uncooked, bagels, homemade ice cream and pastries, as well as cafés and Caviston's deli.

Moore Street Market
Moore Street; Mon–Sat; bus: 10a, 14a, 46a, Luas: Jervis; map p.132 B2
For a taste of a traditional, old-fashioned Dublin market, pay a visit to Moore Street. An integral part of Dublin's culture, street traders banter while selling their inexpensive fruit, vegetables and flowers.

The SuperNatural Food Market
St Andrew's Resource Centre, Pearse Street; tel: 01 677 2255; www.supernatural.ie; Sat 9.30am–3.30pm; bus: 50, 77, 77a, DART: Pearse
This is the 'greenest of green' markets, an environmentally friendly, sustainable and locally sourced market offering organic products of fine quality. Wander through a range of food stalls, including an organic butcher, a fishmonger and a master baker.

FOOD AND DRINK SHOPS
Avoca
11 Anne Street South; tel: 01 677 4215; www.avoca.ie; Mon–Sat 10am–6pm, Thur until 8pm, Sun 11am–6pm; bus: 10a, 128, 736; map p.136 C3
For a gorgeous array of tasty Irish produce take a

Right: Jameson whiskey makes a good souvenir or gift to take home.

look at Avoca's food hall, located in the basement of this department store. Fresh breads, cakes, salads and much more are a visual feast for the eyes.

Celtic Whiskey Shop
27–28 Dawson Street; tel: 01 675 9744; www.celticwhiskeyshop.com; Mon–Sat 10.30am–8pm, Sun 12.30pm–6pm; bus: 10a, 128, 736; map p.137 C3
This shop has the best selection of Irish whiskeys in town, together with varieties from Scotland and around the world, many rare and collecta-

ble. At No. 28 there is a good selection of wines, gourmet foods and chocolates.

Fallon & Byrne
11–17 Exchequer Street; tel: 01 472 1010; www.fallonand byrne.net; Mon–Fri 8am–10pm, Sat 9am–9pm, Sun 11am–8pm; bus: 16a, 19a, 83; map p.136 B4
Alongside a restaurant and wine bar is a delectable organic food hall. The freshest of beautifully displayed fruit and vegetables, locally sourced meats, sinful cakes and much more are on offer.

A new Italian quarter has evolved on the north side of the River Liffey at Lower Ormond Quay, close to the Jervis Street Luas stop. This shopping and eating district features the deli-cum-wine bar Enoteca delle Langhe (*see Bars and Cafés, p.37*) and Wallace's Italian Food Shop. Here you will find scrumptious fresh bread, Italian cheeses, salsa, pasta and olive oils.

Mitchell & Son Wine Merchants
chq Building, IFSC, Docklands; tel: 01 612 5540; www.mitchel landson.com; Mon–Fri 10.30am–7pm, Sat 11am–6pm; bus: 53a, 151, Luas: Georges Dock; map p.133 E2
Established in 1805, this wine merchant has moved to the sparkling new chq building in the developing Dockland district. Renowned for its exclusive vintages, the family company imports and distributes fine wines from around the world.

Sheridans Cheese Shop
11–13 Suffolk Street; tel: 01 679 3143; www.sheridans cheesemongers.com; Mon–Sat 10am–6pm, Thur until 7.30pm; bus: 10a, 13a, 15a; map p.136 C4
A mouth-watering experience awaits in this glorious shop packed to the rafters with massive blocks of cheese, primarily Irish but now stocking a full range of European cousins of the highest quality. Also delectable Irish produce including salmon, jams and marmalades.

Left: Irish coffee... and some regular espresso for when it all gets too much.

G

Gay and Lesbian

With the major changes in Dublin's demographics and its developing social life in the last two decades, the city's gay and lesbian scene has also seen unprecedented growth. With one of the highest youth populations in Europe, the expansion in nightlife in general has been phenomenal, and there are now several dedicated gay venues located on a strip from Capel Street to the north of the river to South Great George's Street to the south, via Parliament Street in Temple Bar. An increasing number of clubs, pubs and bars also have solely gay nights at least one day of the week.

GAY AND LESBIAN ORGANISATIONS AND WEBSITES

Gay Ireland

www.gay-ireland.com
This dedicated website gives lots of information and links about the gay and lesbian social scene in Dublin, as well as Ireland in general.

Gay Switchboard Dublin

Tel: 01 872 1055;
www.gayswitchboard.ie;
Mon–Thur 7.30–9.30pm
A team of volunteers have been running this service for over 30 years. Call if you have any problems, or check out the website. Note this is for serious issues only, not a general information line.

OUThouse

105 Capel Street; tel: 01 873 4932; www.outhouse.ie; daily check for times; bus: 37, 39a, 70a, Luas: Jervis; map p.132 A1
This is Dublin's social and resource centre for the gay and lesbian community, formed in 1994, which now has as many as 1,000

The *Gay Community News* is Ireland's longest-running gay and lesbian publication (www.gcn.ie), providing both serious rights- and community-based information, as well as listings, articles, classifieds, film and book reviews and lifestyle features. A monthly free sheet, it is available from Waterstones, Books Upstairs, Tower Records, Juice and other city centre locations. *See also Literature, p.77.*

people dropping in each week. The centre offers all kinds of relevant advice and information, as well as a programme of events and details of what's on in the city. There is also a library and internet access.
    The **outhouse@105 Café** (daytime: Mon–Fri 1.30–5.30pm, Sat 1–5pm (all welcome); evenings: Tue 6.30–9.30pm (all welcome), Thur 7–10pm (women only), Fri 7–10pm (men only)) is a popular meeting place.

QID

www.queerid.com

An excellent website which gives information of events, club nights and gay and lesbian helplines.

CLUBS AND BARS
The Dragon

89 South Great George's Street; tel: 01 487 1590; www.capital bars.com; bar: daily 5pm until late, club: Mon, Wed–Sat 10pm–2.30am, Sun 5pm–11pm; bus: 16a, 19a, 83; map p.136 B3
One of Dublin's newest gay disco bars, the Dragon

Right: at Dublin's foremost gay bar, The George.

meeting new people. You need to check out in advance what's on, as themes constantly change.

FESTIVALS
Dublin Pride Festival
www.dublinpride.org
Held In June, this is an annual two-week celebration of gay life in Ireland. The festival culminates in the Gay Pride march through the city centre, a riot of colour and a cacophony of sound, and a serious message of gay solidarity against discrimination. Check out the website for all the details.

GAZE
www.gaze.ie
GAZE is the title for the Dublin International Lesbian & Gay Film Festival. The festival offers an exciting programme, packed with premières, new independent features, documentaries, shorts, award winners and experimental films over the August bank holiday weekend at the Lighthouse Cinema in Smithfield.
SEE ALSO FILM, P.57

Left: celebrating at Pride.

has been revamped into a stylish, intimate venue.

The George
89 South Great George's Street; tel: 01 487 1590; www.capital bars.com; Mon–Tue 12.30pm–11.30pm, Wed–Sat 12.30pm–2.30am, Sun 12.30pm–1am; bus: 16a, 19a, 83; map p.136 B3
One of Ireland's oldest gay bars and clubs, which paved the way for a freer lifestyle for the gay community in Dublin.

Check out the Old Bar known as Jurassic Park for a drink or hit the Dance Bar and Club, which draws a young and trendy gay crowd.

Pantibar
7–8 Capel Street; tel: 01 874 0710; www.pantibar.com; daily from 5pm; bus: 37, 39a, 70a; Luas: Jervis; map p.132 A1
Re-styled from the bar Gubu, the Pantibar is described as funky and fun, glamorous, and at times outrageous. The weekends are all about dancing and

History

4th century BC
The Celts land in Ireland and stamp their authority and culture on early inhabitants.

5th century AD
The Christian faith is established. St Patrick plays a pivotal role in converting the Celtic people.

AD841
The Vikings establish a trading station near present-day Kilmainham. They move downstream to the area around Dublin Castle in the 10th century.

1014
High King Brian Boru defeats the Dublin Vikings at the Battle of Contarf.

1169
The Norman barons, led by Richard de Clare (known as Strongbow), invade Dublin, which is conquered the following year.

1171
Henry II grants the city a charter and establishes a court. Despite numerous rebellions, the city stays in English hands for the following 700 years.

1180
Christ Church Cathedral is built; St Patrick's Cathedral is founded in 1192, receiving cathedral status in 1219.

1348–51
The Black Death arrives in Ireland for the first time. Dubliners are buried in mass graves in an area still known as Blackpitts.

1534
Henry VIII's army quashes a rebellion by 'Silken'

Thomas Fitzgerald. Dublin is declared an Anglican city in 1537.

1592
Queen Elizabeth I grants a royal charter for the founding of Trinity College.

1690
Protestant William of Orange triumphs at the Battle of the Boyne.

1713
The writer Jonathon Swift is ordained as Cathedral Dean of St Patrick's, a position he holds until his death in 1745.

1714
Start of the Georgian era, Dublin's great period of classical architecture.

1742
The first performance of Handel's *Messiah* takes place on 13 April. Dublin blossoms as a cultural centre.

1745
Leinster House is built by the Earl of Kildare, which

POBLACHT NA H EIREANN.

THE PROVISIONAL GOVERNMENT

OF THE

IRISH REPUBLIC

TO THE PEOPLE OF IRELAND.

leads to the new elite building in the same area; today it is known as the Georgian District.

1759
The Guinness Brewery is founded.

1782
The Irish Parliament secures legislative independence from Britain.

1798
An abortive French-backed attempt at rebellion by Dubliner Wolfe Tone takes place.

1800
The Act of Union sees the Irish Parliament dissolved and direct rule is reinstated from Westminster.

1829
Daniel O'Connell implements the Catholic Emancipation Act and becomes known as 'The Liberator'.

1845–9
The Great Potato Famine – soup kitchens are set up throughout the city. One million people die and many others flee the country for America.

1890s
The Celtic Revival movement sees a resurgence and pride in all things Irish.

1900
Queen Victoria visits Dublin.

1916
The Easter Rising – many rebels incarcerated and executed in Kilmainham Gaol.

1920
The first Bloody Sunday, as 11 people are killed by British forces.

1922
Civil war is declared. British forces evacuate Dublin Castle.

1949
The Republic of Ireland is declared.

1963
President John F. Kennedy makes a state visit to the city.

1979
Pope John Paul II says mass in Phoenix Park to more than 1.3 million people.

1991
Mary Robinson sweeps to victory as the first female president.

1998
Voters in referendums approve the Good Friday Agreement in the Republic of Ireland and in Northern Ireland.

2002
The Irish punt is replaced by the euro; prices rise as Dublin's economy, known as the 'Celtic Tiger', booms.

2004
Ireland introduces a no-smoking policy in enclosed public places.

2009
Despite the recession, which bites hard, the redevelopment of Dublin's Docklands continues.

Hotels

F rom boutique hotels to sheer luxury to endless chain hotels, the variety when choosing where to stay in Dublin is never a problem, although the cost could be. Undoubtedly it is expensive here compared to some other European cities, although this can vary depending on where you stay; north of the river is generally cheaper than south, for instance. Dublin is extremely popular, and it is advisable to reserve a room in advance. There are self-catering options, but these are mostly located in the suburbs or on the coast. However, the standard of hostels in the city is very good and worth considering if you are on a tight budget.

FAR WEST AND PHOENIX PARK
Best Western Ashling Hotel
Parkgate Street; tel: 01 677 2324; www.ashlinghotel.ie; €; bus: 748, Luas Heuston; map p.130 B1
After major refurbishment, the contemporary surroundings of this large chain hotel go that bit fur-

ther than the average Best Western establishment, and the rates are still very good value. Some rooms have views over the River Liffey.

Best Western Sheldon Park
Kylemore Road; tel: 01 460 1055; www.sheldonpark.ie; €; bus: 747
Extensive leisure facilities, including an indoor pool and spa, are a soothing sight when visitors return to the suburbs after a long hard day exploring the city. The restaurant creates a lovely setting for excellent traditional Irish cuisine.

Hilton Dublin Kilmainham
Inchicore Road, Kilmainham; tel: 01 420 1800; www.hilton.co.uk/dublinkil mainham; €€; bus: 59b, 78a, 79
New in 2007, this hotel's colourful, chic surroundings are sure to impress at this price level. Soak your tired muscles in the hydrotherapy pool, relax in the sauna or enjoy a cock-

tail before dining at the brasserie restaurant.

SOUTH OF THE LIFFEY, WEST
Arlington Hotel
Lord Edward Street; tel: 01 670 8777; www.arlingtonhoteltem plebar.com; €; bus: 50, 56a, 123; map p.136 A4
An old favourite on the doorstep of Temple Bar, formerly the Parliament, this hotel has undergone extensive refurbishment – although the distinctive exterior remains just the same. Legends bar comes alive most nights, when Irish dancing dinner shows take place. Rates include breakfast.

Harding Hotel
Copper Alley, Fishamble Street; tel: 01 679 6500; www.hard inghotel.ie; €€; bus: 50, 56a, 123; map p.136 A4
Guests are greeted with a smile at this small hotel on a secluded cobbled street opposite Christ Church

A Dublin institution and national treasure, the **Shelbourne** (27 St Stephen's Green; tel: 01 663 4500; www.theshel bourne.ie; €€€€; bus: 92, 118, 746; map p.137 C2) is worth visiting for the afternoon tea if you can't afford the high prices to stay. Regarded as one of the world's great hotels and beloved by politicians and celebrities, its recent renovation was a great success, retaining its former splendour while upgrading its facilities. Nestle down in Egyptian cotton sheets, pamper yourself in a marble bathroom and dine in a number of first-class restaurants.

Right: The Clarence's glamorous garden terrace.

66

Left: the well-placed Jurys Inn Christchurch.

Price ranges, which are given as a guide only, are for a standard double room with bathroom in peak season, including service and tax but excluding breakfast. Note that it is always worth checking to see if the hotel is offering a promotional deal.

€€€€	over €200
€€€	€150–200
€€	€100–150
€	under €100

Cathedral; Dublin's oldest medieval street, Copper Alley, literally runs through the reception area. Newly renovated in 2007, the bedrooms are individual and decorated in vibrant colours.

Jurys Inn Christchurch
Christchurch Place; tel: 01 454 0000; www.jurysinns.com/jurysinn_christchurch; €; bus: 50, 56a, 123; map p.136 A3
This long-standing favourite still remains one of the most popular hotels in this part of Dublin, purely and simply because it offers good value for money, comfortable and spacious accommodation with the city right on the doorstep.

CENTRAL CORE, SOUTH OF THE LIFFEY
The Clarence
6–8 Wellington Quay; tel: 01 407 0800; www.theclarence.ie; €€; bus: 66a, 66b, 67a; map p.136 A1

The mere fact Bono of U2 fame owns this hotel means The Clarence is popular with celebrities, who often occupy the top-floor penthouse overlooking the Liffey. The hotel flaunts self-indulgence with its leather-clad lifts, rich shades, Irish craftwork, staff fitted out in designer suits and king-size beds dressed with Egyptian cotton.

The Morgan
10 Fleet Street; tel: 01 643 7000; www.themorgan.com; €€–€€€; bus: 46a, 150, 746; map p.136 C4
The epitome of cutting-edge design, this

Left (from top): the swimming pool and a junior suite at the Merrion, and the charming grounds of Number 31.

glam-rock hotel ticks all the boxes. The bedrooms have cool, clean lines, brilliant white spaces and funky furnishings. Opt for a top-floor room to avoid the Temple Bar noise, which continues into the early hours.

Temple Bar Hotel

Fleet Street; tel: 01 612 9200; www.templebarhotel.com; €; bus: 46a, 150, 746; map p.136 A1

For party animals looking to fall out of their hotel into the Temple Bar hubbub, this modern hotel provides a good standard, efficient service and spacious bedrooms at a reasonable price that includes breakfast.

The Westbury Hotel

Grafton Street; tel: 01 679 1122; www.doylecollection.com; €€€; bus: 10a, 14a, 70b; map p.136 C3

It doesn't come better than the Westbury, one of the city's most exclusive hotels, with its fair share of rich and famous sleeping in the sophisticated guest rooms. Five-star touches stretch to TV screens in the bathroom. With the hotel's striking presence on Grafton Street, highly convenient for the some of the city's best shopping, what more could one want?

ST STEPHEN'S GREEN AND AROUND

Conrad Dublin

Earlsfort Terrace; tel: 01 602 8900; http://conrad hotels1.hilton.com; €€€; bus: 14a, 15a, 746; map p.137 C1

If you're in town for the

classical music, stay at this five-star hotel facing the beautiful National Concert Hall *(see Music, p.90)*. Contemporary and refined, the bedrooms have plenty of space. A short walk from St Stephen's Green, there are many excellent restaurants in the vicinity.

Fitzwilliam Hotel
St Stephen's Green; tel: 01 478 7000; www.fitzwilliamhotel.com; €€€; bus: 92, 118, 746; map p.136 C2
This Terence Conran-designed hotel exudes exuberant shades, and boasts a restaurant where the food is created by the Michelin-starred chef Kevin Thornton. For the perfect view, request a room overlooking St Stephen's Green or the courtyard garden.
SEE ALSO RESTAURANTS, P.101

Number 31
31 Leeson Close; tel: 01 676 5011; www.number31.ie; €€€; bus: 11, 78, 118; map p.137 D1
Georgian townhouse meets retro coach house at this hotel run by the perfect host. Life centres around a sunken lounge, and the 21 bedrooms are fitted with French antiques and large sumptuous beds. An amazing breakfast is included in the rate.

Price ranges, which are given as a guide only, are for a standard double room with bathroom in peak season, including service and tax but excluding breakfast. Note that it is always worth checking to see if the hotel is offering a promotional deal.

€€€€	over €200
€€€	€150–200
€€	€100–150
€	under €100

Staunton's on the Green
St Stephen's Green; tel: 01 478 2300; www.thecastlehotel group.com; €€; bus: 14a, 15a, 128; map p.136 C2
Floor-to-ceiling windows in the bedrooms offer wonderful views over the green or the garden to the rear, a charming feature at this Georgian guesthouse with plenty of character. In a fabulous location close to the city's major museums.

GEORGIAN DISTRICT AND MUSEUMS
Buswells Hotel
23–25 Molesworth Street; tel: 01 614 6500; www.buswells.ie; €; bus: 10a, 128, 746; map p.137 C3
Made up of two Georgian townhouses, this is one of Dublin's longest-serving hotels and one of the friendliest, where a real Irish charm has been retained. The bedrooms are small and quaint, but that adds to the charm.

Merrion Hotel
Upper Merrion Street; tel: 01 603 0600; www.merrionhotel.com; €€€; bus: 172; map p.137 D2
Four Georgian houses set around a pretty garden make up this exquisite hotel that represents the epitome of polished finery. Rooms reflect the 18th-century period and have lavish marble bathrooms. Spoil your taste buds in the renowned Patrick Guilbaud Restaurant.
SEE ALSO RESTAURANTS, P.101

O'Callaghan Alexander Hotel
Merrion Square; tel: 01 607 3700; www.ocallaghan hotels.com; €€; bus: 45; map p.137 E3
An elegant corner building

There are a good variety of hostels on offer in Dublin; for a selection, check out **www.hostelsdublin.com**. To be right in the action in Temple Bar, try **Oliver St John Gogarty Hostel** (18–21 Anglesea Street; tel: 01 671 1822; www.gogar tys.ie; €; bus: 50, 56a, 123; map p.136 A4), which provides good, clean accommodation and a free breakfast; traditional music can be heard at the adjoining Gogarty's pub. Also close to Temple Bar is lively **Kinlay House** (2–12 Lord Edward Street; tel: 01 679 6644; www.kinlayhouse.ie; €; bus: 92, 118, 746; map p.136 A4), which is safe and clean and offers a free breakfast in the price, plus free internet and Wifi access.

---

distinguished by its large bay windows and stone round-tower entrance. Another fine hotel from the O'Callaghan stable, this one has a more contemporary interior than its sister hotel *(see below)*, but is equally as good.

O'Callaghan Davenport Hotel
Merrion Square; tel: 01 607 3500; www.ocallaghanhotels.com;

Below: a stylist reflection at the Fitzwilliam.

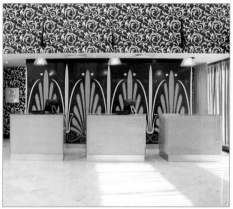

€€; bus: 45; map p.137 D3
Dating back to 1863, this landmark building originally served as a gospel house before being transformed into a stylish hotel, which is beautifully presented, inside and out. The hotel stands in a lovely, quiet spot on Merrion Square.

DOCKLANDS AND CANALS
Clarion Hotel IFSC
IFSC; tel: 01 433 8800; www.clarionhotelifsc.com; €€–€€€; bus: 53a, 151, train: Connolly, Luas: Georges Dock; map p.133 E1
The Clarion may be located in the financial district, but it's a good choice for tourists and families, too. Its stylish, contemporary rooms are

Price ranges, which are given as a guide only, are for a standard double room with bathroom in peak season, including service and tax but excluding breakfast. Note that it is always worth checking to see if the hotel is offering a promotional deal.

€€€€	over €200
€€€	€150–200
€€	€100–150
€	under €100

uncluttered and calm, the perfect antidote to the city's bustle. There is an excellent health and fitness centre.

Grand Canal Hotel
Upper Grand Canal Street; tel: 01 646 1000; €; www.grand canalhotel.com; bus: 5, 7, 45, DART: Grand Canal Dock
You don't always have to pay a fortune in Dublin to get a good contemporary hotel with spacious rooms and helpful staff such as this. A pleasant 15-minute walk gets you to the city centre, but the DART is on your doorstep if needed.

Jurys Inn Custom House
Custom House Quay; tel: 01 829 0400; www.jurysinns.com; €–€€€; bus: 53a, 151, train: Connolly, Luas: George's Dock; map p.133 E1
The dependable Jurys' chain has been serving Dublin for over 100 years, and this particular hotel is set right among the up and coming Docklands district and overlooks the Liffey.

Maldron Hotel
Cardiff Lane, Sir John Roger-son's Quay; tel: 01 643 9500;

www.maldronhotels.com; €€; bus: 3
Part of the splendid new river and Docklands development, this hotel is bang in the centre of things. It's contemporary and spacious and close to good restaurants and nightlife, yet not too far from all the traditional city attractions.

Mespil Hotel
Mespil Road; tel: 01 488 4600; www.mespilhotel.com; €–€€; bus: 746; map p.137 E1
The Mespil occupies a quiet spot near the Grand Canal, but is only a bus ride or 10-minute walk from the centre. It's in a perfect location for those wanting to escape the bustle of central Dublin.

NORTH OF THE LIFFEY, WEST
Maldron Hotel Smithfield
Smithfield; tel: 01 485 0900; www.maldronhotels.com; €€; bus: 66, 83, Luas: Smithfield; map p.131 E2
If you stay at this hotel ask for one of the rooms that

Right: the vibrant restaurant at the Morrison.

Left: contemporary style at the Maldron Hotel.

The first 'boutique' hotel in Dublin, the Morrison still retains its style. The bedrooms have clean lines and invoke calm, whereas the public areas are more flamboyant and colourful. Round off your day with cocktails or relax in the spa.

O'CONNELL STREET AND BEYOND
Best Western Premier Academy Plaza
10–14 Findlater Place, off Upper O'Connell Street; tel: 01 878 0666; www.academy plazahotel.ie; €€; bus: 16a, 41, 746; map p.132 C3

After a complete overhaul, the comfortable Academy Plaza is well placed for all the major tourist attractions and the newly developed Docklands district. Check for excellent deals, including an evening meal and full Irish breakfast.

For those who prefer to be independent and have more space, **Stephen's Hall Suites** (14–17 Lower Leeson Street; tel: 01 638 1111; www.premiersuites dublin.com; €–€€€; bus: 11, 118, 746; map p.137 D1) benefits from the privacy of an apartment but the atmosphere of a hotel. It's like home away from home; each suite has a kitchen fully equipped with appliances such as a dishwasher, and a living area with a 32in plasma TV and hi-fi stereo.

Cassidys Hotel
6–8 Cavendish Row; tel: 01 878 0555; www.cassidyshotel.com; €€; bus: 16a, 41, 746; map p.132 B3

Located just off the end of O'Connell Street in three converted Georgian houses, this family-owned hotel offers modern accommodation with a traditional personal touch. The hotel is close to the contemplative Garden of Remembrance, perfect for unwinding after a day of sightseeing.

features wall-to-ceiling glass windows or with a balcony for some great views of the city. For a 360-degree panorama over Dublin, take a trip up the Chimney on the other side of the Plaza.

Morrison Hotel
Ormond Quay; tel: 01 887 2400; www.morrisonhotel.ie; €€–€€€€; bus: 25a, 66a, 67a; map p.132 B1

Above: decadent style at the Dylan Hotel.

The Gresham
23 Upper O'Connell Street; tel: 01 878 7966; www.gresham-hotels.com; €€€–€€€€; bus: 14a, 16a, 746; map p.132 C2
This landmark Dublin hotel has been refurbished and is one of the best and most luxurious in the city. It has long been a favourite meeting place for its traditional afternoon tea and is particularly noted for its excellent attentive service. Be sure to check for some good online deals.

Hotel St George
Parnell Square East; tel: 01 874 5611; www.thecastlehotel group.com; €€; bus: 1, 2, 14a; map p.132 B3
With a bar overlooking the peaceful Garden of Remembrance, this attractive Georgian hotel

Price ranges, which are given as a guide only, are for a standard double room with bathroom in peak season, including service and tax but excluding breakfast. Note that it is always worth checking to see if the hotel is offering a promotional deal.

€€€€	over €200
€€€	€150–200
€€	€100–150
€	under €100

offers a comfortable stay with good facilities in a traditional, friendly ambience. A hearty breakfast is included in the price.

BALLSBRIDGE AND AROUND
Bewley's Hotel Ballsbridge
Merrion Road, Ballsbridge; tel: 01 668 1111; www.bewleys hotels.com/ballsbridge; €–€€; bus: 5, 7, 45, DART: Sandymount
An old favourite in the city, Bewley's have created a comfortable, efficient hotel within an impressive old Masonic school building. It is close to the RDS Showgrounds, has efficient public transport to the city and is ideally placed for quick access to the coast, making it a good place for families to stay.

Dylan Hotel
Eastmorland Place, Ballsbridge; tel: 01 660 3000; www.dylan.ie; €€€€; bus: 5, 7, 45
If you can push the boat out, this is a fabulous place to stay. The interior of the Victorian building has been transformed with an ultra-modern, edgy design of superb quality, with a twist of Rococo elegance. The modern wing sits comfortably alongside, its cutting-edge exterior mirroring the original. There is also a lovely outdoor terrace for coffee or drinks.

Merrion Hall
54 Merrion Road, Ballsbridge; tel: 01 283 8155; www.halpin sprivatehotels; €€€; bus: 5, 7, 45, DART: Sandymount
Located opposite the RDS Showgrounds, this

redeveloped Edwardian guesthouse makes a pleasant change to staying at a conventional hotel. The comfortable and peaceful public rooms provide a welcome retreat and the bedrooms are spacious and well equipped. An award-winning breakfast is included in the price.

Pembroke Townhouse
90 Pembroke Road, Ballsbridge; tel: 01 660 0277; www.pembroketownhouse.ie; €€; bus: 5, 7, 45
There's a great mix of Georgian elegance and contemporary style at this superior guesthouse. A full buffet breakfast is included, plus traditional cooked Irish to order.

Right: the grand dining room at Bewley's Hotel Ballsbridge.

Left: the inviting entrance to the Merrion Hotel *(see p.69).*

www.schoolhousehotel.com; €€; bus: 5, 7, 45

A full Irish breakfast is included in the price at this trendy small hotel, located close to the Grand Canal. The unique building has been transformed internally to provide spacious bedrooms, all named after Irish writers. The high-ceilinged adjoining restaurant offers a selection of French and modern Irish dishes.

BEYOND DUBLIN
Ghan House
Ghan Huse, Carlingford, Co. Louth; tel: 0402 937 3682; www.ghanhouse.com; €

If you want to get out of the city for a night or two, this gorgeous 18th-century house is just an hour away. With only 12 rooms, this homely family-run hotel is operated to a high standard, and the views across the Lough and the Mountains of Mourne are stunning. There is a delicious breakfast included in the price, an excellent restaurant and a cookery school.

Woodenbridge Hotel and Lodge
Vale of Avoca, Arklow; tel: 04 02 35146; www.woodenbridge hotel.com; €€

This hotel, in the Best Western chain, is superbly located between Avoca and Arklow and set in beautiful scenery. Popular for weddings and with golfers, it is the perfect base for touring County Wicklow or spending a few days outside the city. Breakfast included.

If you're looking for 4 or 5-star accommodation, exclusive hotels in Dublin can be very expensive, particularly at weekends, when the rates go sky-high. It is worth considering staying further out in the more relaxing suburbs, where the room tariffs are better value for money. Ballsbridge is a pleasant, quiet area that has several 4-star establishments at 3-star prices. But remember, it will mean a short bus or taxi ride into the city.

Some bedrooms are on the small side, but cleanliness and presentation is of a high standard.

Schoolhouse Hotel
2–8 Northumberland Road; Ballsbridge; tel: 01 667 5014;

I

Irish Design

For many centuries Dublin has upheld a reputation as a centre of creative excellence. Georgian silver and Irish furniture embody some of the finest craftsmanship of the late 18th and early 19th centuries – look for the harp in the hallmark that indicates it was made in Ireland. Today, traditional Irish design has a modern edge. Many shops and outlets are full of the work of Irish craftspeople and fashion designers who have turned their hand to other interesting challenges, from furniture and jewellery to beautiful items in stone, wood, glass and other natural materials, in both traditional and contemporary styles.

MADE IN IRELAND

Fashion stores carry contemporary, alternative and classic collections from several local designers who have contributed to the world of fashion. Those to watch out for are Ireland's most famous fashion designer, **Paul Costelloe**, and the internationally renowned designer **Louise Kennedy**. Check out **Vivienne Walsh's** intricate costume jewellery, **Orla Kiely's** handbags, **Slim Barrett's** fairy-tale tiaras (Victoria Beckham wore one of his during her marriage to David Beckham) and **Lainey Keogh's** knitwear.

If you're looking for something of contemporary Ireland for your home, consider **John Rocha's** minimalist glass range that brought **Waterford Crystal** into the 21st century. Hand-blown **Jerpoint** glass is instantly recognisable by its simple design with strong colour bursts that add subtle colour to a

Above: whimsical designs at Avoca.

room. Orla Kiely's bold, girly patterns liven up kitchen items such as mugs, tea towels and storage boxes. **Nicholas Mosse's** sponged pottery stands out from the rest, and **Louis Mulcahy** is one of Ireland's most prolific ceramic designers.

IRISH DESIGN SHOPPING

Avoca
11–13 Suffolk Street; tel: 01 677 4215; www.avoca.ie; Mon–Wed, Fri 10am–6pm, Thur 10am–8pm, Sat 10am–6.30pm, Sun 11am–6pm; bus: 10a, 13a, 15a; map p.136 C4

Avoca may have started out in 1723 weaving fabrics, but they now offer a huge range of their own Irish crafts at this department store, combining the traditional with contemporary style.
SEE ALSO BARS AND CAFÉS, P.35; BEYOND DUBLIN, P.24

Blarney Woollen Mills
21–23 Nassau Street; tel: 01 451 6111; www.blarney.com; Mon–Sat 9am–6pm,Sun 11am–6pm; bus: 10a, 13a, 15a; map p.137 C4

Don't be fooled by the

74

Still in its infancy, Temple Bar's outdoor **Designer Mart** at Cow's Lane showcases over 30 innovative artists and designers from around the country, an ideal place to pick up a one-off piece from the creator. The market operates every Saturday from 10am until 5pm and offers a wide selection from jewellery, fashion and furniture to visual art and photography.

name; most other traditional Irish crafts can be found here as well: crystal, china, jewellery, line and lots more.

Cleo

18 Kildare Street; tel: 01 676 1421; www.irishclothing.ie; Mon–Sat 9am–5.30pm; bus: 10a, 14a, 15a; map.137 C3
A small outlet specialising in one-off hand-knitted sweaters made from natural fibres.

DESIGNYARD

48–49 Nassau Street; tel: 01

Right: Irish design extends even to lamp posts.

474 1011; www.designyard.ie; Mon–Sat 10am–6.30pm, Thur until 8pm; bus: 10a, 13a, 15a; map p.136 C4
DESIGNYARD showcases imaginative designs in jewellery, sculpture, ceramics, wood, glass and metalwork from some of Ireland's hottest new talents.

House of Ireland

38 Nassau Street; tel: 01 671 1111; www.house ofireland.com; Mon–Sat 9am–6pm, Thur until 8pm, Sun

Left: homeware at Avoca.

10.30–5.30; bus: 10a, 13a, 15a; map p.136 C4
The best of Irish giftware is found on the shelves here, including glass from John Rocha and Louise Kennedy, china from Belleek and Genesis figurines.

Kevin & Howlin

31 Nassau Street; tel: 01 677 0257; www.kevinandhowlin.com; Mon–Sat 9.30am–5.30pm; bus: 10a, 13a, 15a; map p.136 C4
Irish tweed is the focal point here, hand-woven by Magees in Donegal for this family-run tailor, which has been in business since 1933.

Louis Mulcahy

46 Dawson Street; tel: 01 670 9311; Mon–Sat 9.30am–5.30pm; bus: 10a, 128, 746; map p.137 C3
A charming little shop that features the signature pottery of Louis Mulcahy, who still uses traditional methods of throwing pots and applying the rich shades freehand using a brush.

Literature

The contribution of Irish authors, poets and playwrights to world literature is quite outstanding. Dubliner James Joyce even has his own day, 'Bloomsday', on 16 June, when dedicated fans follow in the steps of *Ulysses* hero Leopold Bloom. The literary legacy list is phenomenal, including Swift, Wilde, Shaw, Yeats, O'Casey, Beckett, Kavanagh and Behan. Modern writers have continued the literary tradition, with the likes of Seamus Heaney, Brian Friel, Edna O'Brien, Roddy Doyle and Frank McCourt. Visit the Dublin Writers Museum *(see Museums and Galleries, p.87)* to learn about their lives and works.

LITERARY GREATS

Jonathan Swift (1667–1745)

Swift wrote with the wit and satire that epitomises a whole genre of Irish literature. It is ironical that his *Gulliver's Travels* (1726) is a considered a children's classic, as it is full of political satire and nuance.

William Butler Yeats (1865–1939)

Regarded as the greatest lyrical poet Ireland has produced, Yeats was the first Irishman to win a Nobel Prize, in 1923. His highly regarded works include *The Tower* (1928).

James Joyce (1882–1941)

Joyce wrote four iconic works among his repertoire – *Dubliners* (1914), *A Portrait of the Artist as a Young Man* (1916), *Ulysses* (1922) and *Finnegans Wake* (1939), which progress in difficulty. Find out all about him at the **James Joyce Centre**.

SEE ALSO MUSEUMS AND GALLERIES, P.89

Samuel Beckett (1906–1989)

Winner of a Nobel Prize in 1969, Beckett is most famous for his play *Waiting for Godot* (1949). He was, however, also a prolific novelist and poet.

Seamus Heaney (b.1929)

Ireland's most prominent modern poet hails from Northern Ireland, but settled in Dublin in the 1970s. He won a Nobel Prize in 1995.

> How many people know that the famed character of Dracula may well have been conceived in a Dublin suburb? Although Bram Stoker (1847–1912) wrote the novel *Dracula* (1897) while living in London, it was during his childhood in Clontarf, just outside the city, that his interest in stories began. He was bedridden with a mysterious illness until the age of seven, when he made a miraculous recovery, going on to excel as an athlete while a student at Trinity College.

Above: W.B. Yeats.

PLAYWRIGHTS

Many Irish writers, such as Samuel Beckett, have transcended the genres of novel, play or poem. Those at the forefront as playwrights include **Richard Sheridan**, **Oscar Wilde**, **George Bernard Shaw**, who won a Nobel Prize in 1925, **Sean O'Casey** and **Brendan Behan**. Continuing the tradition today are **Brian Friel**, the controversial **Tom Murphy** and young **Conor McPherson**.

SEE ALSO THEATRE AND DANCE, P.116

Left: Oscar Wilde.

has been serving customers for eight generations. It stocks around 60,000 titles over four floors and specialises in Irish titles, fiction and academic books.

Hughes & Hughes
St Stephen's Green Shopping Centre; tel: 01 478 3060; www.hughesbooks.com; Mon–Sat 9.30am–7pm, Thur until 8pm, Sun 11am–6pm; bus: 92, 118, 746; map p.136 B3
There are six branches of Hughes & Hughes, including this branch in central Dublin. Attentive service gets you that book you really want. Irish literature and travel are well represented.

Waterstones
7 Dawson Street; tel: 01 672 9932; www.waterstones.com; daily 9am–7pm; bus: 10a, 128, 746; map p.137 C3
The bonus of this branch of the well-known bookshop is the excellent Readers Café. Great range of titles, plus events and readings programme. There is another branch in the Jervis Shopping Centre.

BOOKSHOPS
Cathach Books
10 Duke Street; tel: 01 671 8676; www.rarebooks.ie; Mon–Sat 9.30am–5.45pm; bus: 10a, 14a, 70b; map p.136 C3
Cathach specialises in books of Irish interest, with particular emphasis on 20th-century Irish literature and first editions. It leads the field in antiquarian books.

Chapters Bookstore
Ivy Exchange, Parnell Street; tel: 01 872 3297; www.chapters.ie; Mon–Sat 9.30am–6.30pm, Thur until 8pm, Sun noon–6.30pm; bus: 14a, 16a, 746; map p.132 B2
Browse a good range of books, CDs and DVDs, both new and second-hand, at this bookshop set over two floors. There are lots of bargains on offer.

Easons
40 Lower O'Connell Street; tel: 01 858 3800; www.easons.ie; Mon–Sat 8.30am–6.45pm, Thur until 8.45pm, Fri until 7.45pm, Sun noon–5.45pm; bus: 10a, 14a, 46a; map p.132 C1

An Irish chain with some 45 outlets throughout the country, this branch is Easons's flagship store. Founded in 1819, Easons sells a large range of magazines and newspapers, as well as books.

Hodges Figgis
56–58 Dawson Street; tel: 01 677 4754; Mon–Fri 9am–7pm, Thur until 8pm, Sat 9am–6pm, Sun noon–6pm; bus: 10a, 128, 746; map p.137 C3
This is Dublin's oldest and largest bookshop, which

Below: a display at the Dublin Writers Museum.

Museums and Galleries

There is a plethora of interesting museums and galleries to explore in Dublin. These range from fine national institutions covering archaeology, history and art to small individual collections. Lovers of Irish literature will not be disappointed either, with the shrines to such esteemed literati as James Joyce and George Bernard Shaw open for viewing. For a literal taste of Dublin visit the Guinness Storehouse, and for world-beating book archives there is the superb Chester Beatty Library and the Book of Kells.

FAR WEST AND PHOENIX PARK

Guinness Storehouse

St James's Gate; tel: 01 404 4800; www.guinness-store house.com; daily 9.30am–5pm, July–Aug until 7pm; admission charge; bus: 51b, 78a, 123, Luas: James's Street; map p.135 C3

Located in a building steeped in the history of the brewing of Guinness is what can only be described as a giant pint glass, stretching from the ground floor through seven floors to the Gravity Bar *(see Bars and Cafés, p.32)*, high above the city skyline. The floors in between house the exhibitions dedicated to the four basic ingredients needed to create the 'black stuff' – hops, barley, yeast and water. Simple dramatic displays evoke the senses of touch, feel and smell, enhanced with visual dis-plays of old machinery and advertising memorabilia. The experience is topped off with a complimentary glass of Guinness in the Gravity Bar, taken while admiring the view over the city.

Irish Museum of Modern Art

Royal Hospital, Military Road, Kilmainham; tel: 01 612 9900; www.imma.ie; Tue–Sat 10am–5.30pm, Mon from 10.30am, Sun and public hols

Dublin's Best Museums
If time is limited and you want to focus on the city's best museums, then these are the ones to go for:
Art
National Gallery of Ireland *(p.84)*
Dublin City Gallery, The Hugh Lane *(p.87)*
History
National Museum of Ireland, Archaeology *(p.85)*
Dublinia and the Viking World *(p.81)*
Kilmainham Gaol *(p.79)*
Science
Science Gallery, Trinity College *(p.83)*

Below: the Irish Museum of Modern Art.

Left: in the atrium of the Guinness Storehouse.

Jack B. Yeats. Cutting-edge modern artists are also represented, including Damien Hurst and Gilbert and George. There are regularly changing temporary exhibitions held throughout the year.

Kilmainham Gaol

Inchicore Road; tel: 01 435 5984; www.heritageireland.ie; Apr–Sept daily 9.30am–6pm, Oct–Mar Mon–Sat 9.30am–5.30pm, Sun 10am–6pm; admission charge; bus: 59b, 78a, 79

There is a sense of eeri-ness when you enter one of the largest unoccupied prisons in Europe, its stark and severe interior a sharp reminder of the Irish rebels' continuous struggle for freedom against British rule. It opened as a prison in 1796, finally closing in

noon–5.30pm; free; bus: 26, 51, 123, Luas: Heuston; map p.134 A3

The splendid building housing the museum was last used as a hospital in 1927. Some 60 years later, it was transformed and assumed its present title as Ireland's leading national institution for the collection and presenta-tion of modern and con-temporary art and opened in 1991. At present there are some 4,500 works, including those by promi-nent Irish artists such as

Below: Kilmainham Gaol is a reminder of the Irish struggle under British rule.

Visiting museums and galleries is a pleasure, but it can be a tiring experience. Many of Dublin's institutions have first-class cafés, tearooms and restaurants, producing some good meals and snacks. Of particular note is the Silk Road Café at the **Chester Beatty Library** *(see opposite)*, offering a mouth-watering selection of dishes from the Far East (following the food of many of the countries represented in the library) and Ireland. Other museums concentrate on old-fashioned tearooms with homemade cakes and pastries.

1924. The roll call of eminent names is striking – Robert Emmet, Charles Stewart Parnell, Countess Markiewicz, Eamon de Valera – to name a few. Although the gaol had closed in 1910, it was reopened during the 1916 Easter Rising, and many of those who took part were held and executed here. The visit includes a guided tour and an exhibition that highlights the Great Famine of the mid-19th century, the 1916 Easter Rising and the Civil War of the early 1920s.

National Museum of Ireland, Decorative Arts and History

Collins Barracks, Benburb Street; tel: 01 677 7444; www.museum.ie; Tue–Sat 10am–5pm, Sun 2pm–5pm; free; bus: 25, 66, 90, Luas: Museum; map p.131 C1

The museum is housed in the striking Collins Barracks, which closed as a military institution in 1988. The museum was inaugurated as part of Ireland's national museums and opened in 1997, with plans for an ongoing programme of expansion over the 7-hectare (18-acre) site.

The museum covers a wide spectrum of decorative arts, folk culture and the work of Irish artists and craftspeople. It spans social, military and political history presented in an informative and highly visual way. Highlights include the much-travelled Chinese porcelain *Fonthill Vase*, a 2,000-year old Japanese ceremonial bell and a multi-storey clock, whose winding chains extend the height of two floors. Check out the 'Curator's Choice' for

more highlights. Exhibitions include **The Way We Wore**, exploring the impact of fashion on the Irish people.

SOUTH OF THE LIFFEY, WEST
Chester Beatty Library

The Clock Tower Building, Dublin Castle, Dame Street; tel: 01 407 0750; www.cbl.ie; May–Sept Mon–Fri 10am–5pm, Sat 11am–5pm, Sun 1am–5pm, Oct–Apr closed Mon; free; bus: 50, 56a, 123; map p.136 B3

The collection of Sir Alfred Chester Beatty has been described as the finest collection of manuscripts and books made by a private collector in the 20th century. This honorary citizen of Ireland, a successful mining engineer born in New York, devoted part of his life to searching out manuscripts and objets d'art of the highest quality. There are over 6,000 individual items ranging from *c.*2700BC to the 19th century, with objects as diverse as New Testament papyri, woodblock prints from Japan and Burmese painted fairy-tale books.

Right: in the airy Chester Beatty Library.

Dublin Castle

Dame Street; tel: 01 677 7129; www.dublincastle.ie; State Apartments tours: Mon–Fri 10am–4.45pm, Sat–Sun, public hols 2am–4.45pm; admission charge; bus: 50, 56a, 123; map p.136 A4

The primary function of Dublin Castle is to host State occasions, presidential inaugurations and prestigious conferences. This was not always the case, as, despite alterations and fires, the castle on this site was the headquarters of English rule for over 700 years. Tours cover a visit to the State Apartments, Undercroft and Chapel Royal.

Other museums, open to the public (call for times), are the **Garda** (Police) **Museum** and the **Revenue Museum**, as well as the renowned Chester Beatty Library *(see opposite)*.

Dublin City Hall

Dame Street; tel: 01 222 2204; Mon–Fri 10am–5.15pm, Sun, public hols 2pm–5pm; admission charge; bus: 50, 56a, 123; map p.136 B4

The first thing that strikes a visitor to City Hall is the magnificent ceiling in the entrance hall. **The Story of the Capital** exhibition can be found in the atmospheric valuts. It is a multi-media display tracing the evolution of the city and its colourful past from 1170 to the present day.

Left: the National Museum of Ireland, Decorative Arts and History and one of its displays.

Dublinia and the Viking World

St Michael's Hill, Christchurch; tel: 01 679 4611; www.dublinia.ie; daily 10am–5pm; admission charge; bus: 50, 56a, 123; map p.136 A4

One of the most popular attractions in the city, Dublinia first opened in 1993, with the Viking World exhibition added in 2005. The exhibitions, which were upgraded and extended in 2009, aim to bring medieval Dublin to life and show the importance of the Vikings in the development of Dublin's heritage, through the use of reconstructions, artefacts and interactive displays. The latest exhibitions include an interactive archaeology exhibition and seek to explore life on board a Viking warship, burial customs and the looting of monasteries.

SEE ALSO CHILDREN, P.40

Irish Jewish Museum

3–4 Walworth Road; tel: 01 437 1857; May–Sept: Tue, Thur, Sun 11am–3.30pm, Oct–Apr Sun 10.30am–2.30pm; free; bus: 14, 16a, 19

The museum is located in the Portobello area of Dublin that was once home to a vibrant Jewish community. The synagogue, consisting of two adjoining terrace houses, fell into disuse as the Jewish people moved to other suburbs in the city. It now presents a fascinating museum dedicated to the history of Ireland's Jewish community from the mid-19th century to the present day and displays memorabilia, photographs and paintings.

Marsh's Library

St Patrick's Close; tel: 01 454 3511; www.marshlibrary.ie; Mon, Wed–Fri 9.30am–1pm,

Left: an exhibit at the Douglas Hyde Gallery.

among the illustrious architecture of Trinity College, this purpose-built gallery is modern and its content up-to-the-minute and contemporary. Since it opened in 1978 it has had a considerable presence in the Dublin arts scene. Its focus is to promote the works of both Irish and international contemporary artists, which are displayed in regularly changing exhibitions.

Gallery of Photography

Meeting House Square, Temple Bar; tel: 01 671 4654; www.galleryofphotography.ie; Tue–Sat 11am–6pm, Sun 1pm–6pm; free; bus: 50, 66a, 66b; map p.136 A1
This vibrant gallery is Ireland's premier venue for photographic exhibitions. There is a permanent collection of 20th-century Irish artworks and ongoing exhibitions showcasing Irish and international talent. The bookshop stocks Ireland's widest range of

2–5pm, Sat 10am–1pm; admission charge; bus: 50, 56a, 77; map p.136 A2
Sir William Robinson designed this wonderful library, close to St Patrick's Cathedral and the first public library in Ireland, in 1701. It contains some 25,000 printed books spanning the 16th to early 18th centuries and covers a wide range of subjects including theology, medicine, navigation, music and classical literature, most of which were collected by Archbishop Narcissus Marsh. The library consists of a long gallery flanked on either side with dark oak bookcases and has remained unchanged for over 300 years. In addition there are some 300 manuscripts, displayed in glass-fronted cases.

The Shaw Birthplace

33 Synge Street; tel: 01 475 0854; June–Aug Tue–Fri 10am–1pm, 2am–5pm, Sat 2am–5pm; admission charge;

bus: 16, 16a, 19
Celebrate the early life of playwright and essayist George Bernard Shaw (1856–1950) in his childhood home in Synge Street. The neat terrace house has been lovingly restored to its original Victorian setting and features the drawing room where Shaw's mother held her musical evenings. It is a perfect insight into Victorian domestic life and well worth a visit. Look for the plaque on the outside with its simple inscription, 'Author of Many Plays'.
SEE ALSO LITERATURE, P.76

CENTRAL CORE, SOUTH OF THE LIFFEY

Douglas Hyde Gallery

Trinity College, Nassau Street; tel: 01 608 1116; www.douglashydegallery.com; Mon–Fri 11am–6pm, Thur until 7pm, Sat 11am–4.45pm; free; bus: 10a, 13a, 15a, DART: Pearse; map p.137 C4
Despite its location set

Right: a detail from the Book of Kells, at the Old Library.

photographic publications, plus a great selection of unusual postcards.

National Wax Museum
Foster Place, College Green; tel: 01 671 8373; daily 9.30am–7.30pm (last admission 6.45pm), see website for Sun times; admission charge; bus: 10a, 13a, 15a; map p.136 C4

The Wax Museum reopened its doors in summer 2009 after several years searching for a new home in the city. After finally rejecting a move from Parnell Square to Smithfield, it has relocated to Foster Place next door to the Bank of Ireland. Many of the original exhibits remain, but there are some new faces, too. The main section is devoted to the historical and cultural development of Ireland, with a range of famous Irish people, including those involved in the fight for Irish freedom and literary figures such as James

Joyce. Highlights include a panorama depicting the Ice Age to the present day, a science laboratory celebrating some of the best Irish inventors, and of course the Chamber of Horrors, always guaranteed to thrill.

SEE ALSO CHILDREN, P.40

Old Library and Book of Kells, Trinity College
College Green; tel: 01 896 1661; www.tcd.ie; Mon–Sat 9.30am–5pm, Sun 9.30am–4.30pm, Oct–Apr Sun from noon; admission charge; bus: 10a, 13a, 15a, DART: Pearse; map p.137 C4

Thomas Burg's dignified Old Library was built between 1712 and 1732 and is distinguished by its magnificent Long Room, which measures nearly 65m (213ft) and houses in excess of 200,000 books. The phenomenal **Book of Kells** is displayed on the

ground floor of the Old Library building and is one of the most beautifully illuminated manuscripts in the world. The 9th-century Gospel book has been bound in four separate sections and is written on vellum. The pages are turned on a regular basis to protect them from light. Alongside are other important manuscripts such as the books of Durrow and Armagh.

Science Gallery
Trinity College, Pearse Street (enter by Pearse Street gate); tel: 01 896 4091; www.sci encegallery.ie; times vary, check website or phone for

Left: bold works at the Douglas Hyde Gallery.

> It is important to note that many of the museums and galleries have a last admission time often around an hour before closing. The times given in this chapter are the final closing times, and you need to allow yourself plenty of time to guarantee a decent visit.

times of latest exhibition programme, closed Mon; free/admission charge depending on event; bus: 10a, 13a, 15a, DART: Pearse; map p.137 D4

A science museum with a difference, this gallery invites visitors to interact with their exhibitions. This is where you can have your say at the cutting edge of science and technology. Visitors can speak out, put their own views and explore ideas through installations, workshops and events. Exhibitions change regularly, and the gallery is closed for a short time when a new exhibition is installed. This is a fresh approach to science, primarily geared to adults and young adults aged 15 plus.

Temple Bar Gallery and Studios
5–9 Temple Bar; tel: 01 671 0073; www.temple bargallery.com; Tue–Sat 11am–6pm, Thur until 7pm; free; bus: 50, 66a, 66b; map p.136 B1

Temple Bar Gallery is a non-profit-making arts organisation with the sole purpose of showcasing contemporary works of both new and established artists from Ireland and overseas in a wide range of media. The building also contains 30 artists' studios, which are not open to the public.

ST STEPHEN'S GREEN AND AROUND
RHA Gallagher Gallery
15 Ely Place; tel: 01 661 2558; www.royalhiberniangallery.ie; Mon–Sat 11am–7pm, Sun 2pm–5pm; free; bus: 14a, 15a, 128; map p.137 D2

After a major refurbishment, the **Royal Hibernian Academy** has facilities second to none. The remit is to promote both traditional and innovative visual art to the general public. The annual exhibition held in the Gallagher Gallery from late May to late July exhibits recent work by Academicians, invited artists and emerging artists in the disciplines of painting, print,

If you are interested in photography then pay a visit to the **National Photographic Archive** (Meeting House Square; tel: 01 603 0370/0374; www.nli.ie; archive: Mon, Wed and Thur by appointment only, exhibitions: Mon–Fri 10am–5pm, Sat 10am–2pm; free; bus: 50, 66a, 66b; map p.136 A1) in Temple Bar. An outreach centre of the National Library, it offers access to over 600,000 photographs. To view the collection – by appointment only – you have to request a Reader's ticket, which requires two passport photographs and current identification. The ongoing exhibitions are open to the general public.

photography, drawing, sculpture and architecture. You will find that the majority of works exhibited are for sale. There is also an attractive outdoor sculpture courtyard.

GEORGIAN DISTRICT AND MUSEUMS
National Gallery of Ireland
Merrion Square West; tel: 01 661 5133; www.national gallery.ie; Mon–Sat 9.30am–5.30pm, Thur until 8.30pm, Sun noon–5.30pm; free; bus: 45; map p.137 D3

The imposing home of Ireland's National Gallery was built between 1856 and 1864 and houses one of Europe's premier collection of Old Masters, together with a fine representation of Irish art. The collection comprises some 2,500 paintings and a further 10,000 works in different media, including

Left: the Temple Bar Gallery and Studios.

Above: the National Photographic Archive.

high-quality exhibitions. The main exhibitions are often displayed for several years; a recent one is 'Yeats: The Life and Works of William Butler Yeats', on show until 2010. Other exhibitions have included 'Strangers to Citizens: the Irish in Europe 1600–1800'. Among the library's treasures are the 13th-century manuscript *Topographia Hiberniae* by Giraldus Cambrensis, the manuscripts of W.B. Yeats and James Joyce, and the first editions of the works of Jonathan Swift and Oliver Goldsmith.

prints, drawings, sculptures and objets d'art. The **Millennium Wing**, opened in 2002, contains the **Jack B. Yeats Archive Room**, much of which was donated by the Yeats family. Among a host of highlights in the gallery are the following – Titian's *Ecce Homo* (1558), Caravaggio's *The Taking of Christ* (1602), Rembrandt's *Rest on the Flight into Egypt* (1647),

Jack B. Yeats's *A Liffey Swim* (1923) and Picasso's *Still Life with Mandolin* (1924).

National Library

Kildare Street; tel: 01 603 0200; www.nli.ie; exhibitions: Mon–Wed 9.30am–9pm, Thur–Fri 9.30am–5pm, Sat 9.30am–4.30pm; free; bus: 15a, 74a, 92; map p.137 D3

Within the fine building of the National Library there is a section dedicated to

National Museum of Ireland, Archaeology

Kildare Street; tel: 01 677 7444; www.museum.ie; Tue–Sat 10am–5pm, Sun 2pm–5pm; free; bus: 15a, 74a, 92; map p.137 D3

This museum is worth visiting for the building alone, the interior of which is stunning. The glorious rotunda

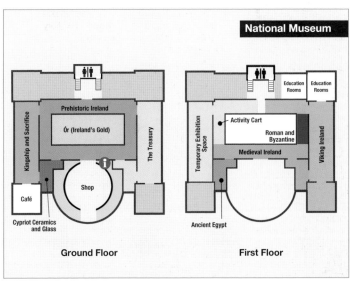

is on the neoclassical design that was so popular at the time. You enter as the servants did, through the basement, and make your way through the rooms of the house to the children's playroom at the top. The intricate detail makes this a unique experience.

DOCKLANDS AND CANALS
Waterways Visitor Centre
Grand Canal Basin; tel, website and times to be confirmed; admission charge; bus: 2, 3, 77
The 'Box on the Docks', as the white cube housing the Visitor Centre is known locally, reopened at the end of 2009 after a major refurbishment and has created a new, dynamic multifunctional space to trace the story of Ireland's inland waterways. Working models and scale models demonstrate how the waterways are managed for both commercial and recreational purposes. The museum is central to the ongoing development of the Grand Canal Dock area.

with its classical columns of marble quarried in Ireland and superb mosaic floors are breathtaking. The massive collection of some 2 million artefacts dates from 7000BC to the late medieval period. On the ground floor the collection of gold work is dazzling, and the exhibition **Ór – Ireland's Gold** is one of the largest and most important in Europe.

On show in the Treasury Rooms are some of the greatest gems of the collection, the 8th-century Tara Brooch, Ardagh Chalice and the Derrynaflan Hoard. Archaeology is well represented in the **Prehistoric Ireland** exhibition, with examples of a bog burial and 4,500-year old long-boat from Lurgan, County

Galway. On the first floor the displays move into the significant Viking period and on through medieval Ireland. **Ancient Egypt** and **Life and Death in the Roman World** show some non-Irish collections.

Number 29
29 Fitzwilliam Street Lower; tel: 01 702 6165; www.esb.ie/no29; Tue–Sat 10am–5pm, Sun noon–5pm; admission charge; bus: 7, 10a, 13a; map p.137 E2
The Electricity Supply Board and the National Museum of Ireland own this wonderful house, and it has been restored meticulously to recapture the original furnishings and atmosphere in the style of the period 1790–1820. The emphasis

NORTH OF THE LIFFEY, WEST
Old Jameson Distillery
Bow Street; tel: 01 807 2355; www.jamesonwhiskey.com; daily 9am–6.30pm, tours every 40 mins; admission charge; bus: 66, 83, Luas: Smithfield; map p.131 E1
Although born in Scotland, John Jameson established his whiskey distillery in Dublin in 1780 and ensured only the best

Right: strolling past the Hugh Lane Gallery.

ingredients were used. He also introduced the concept of triple distillation, which is still practised today. The distillery can only be viewed on a guided tour taking you through exhibits and audiovisual presentations to learn more about the production of *uisce beath*, the Gaelic for 'water of life'. A free sample comes at the end of the tour.

SEE ALSO FOOD AND DRINK, P.59

O'CONNELL STREET AND BEYOND

Dublin City Gallery, The Hugh Lane

Charlemont House, Parnell Square North; tel: 01 222 5550; www.hughlane.ie; Tue–Thur 10am–6pm, Fri–Sat 10am–5pm, Sun 11am–5pm; free; bus: 13, 16, 123; map p.132 B3

The Hugh Lane Gallery perfectly fills a niche between the grand Old Masters at the National Gallery *(see p.84)* and the contemporary art at the Irish Museum of Modern Art *(see p.78)*. For those seeking Impressionist paintings this is the place to go, with wonderful works by the likes of Manet, Monet and Renoir. Highlights include Manet's *La Musique aux Tuileries* (1862), Monet's *Lavacourt sous la Neige* (1881) and Renoir's *Les Parapluies* (1886). Other highlights include the beautiful stained-glass room with the key work by Harry Clarke, *The Eve of St Agnes* (1924), and an amazing reconstruction of the entire studio of Francis Bacon, complete with some 7,500 items. Irish art is well represented, with works by Jack B. and John Butler Yeats and Dublin-born Sir William Orpen.

Sadly, the quirky Natural History Museum in Merrion Street has been closed since July 2007. The plan is for a major restoration of the fabric of the building to ensure a better environment for the exhibits; an extension is also planned. Some 10,000 specimens are being documented and removed from the building. Once funding has been secured, the necessary work should begin, but it may be many years before this fine museum is up and running again.

Dublin Writers Museum

18 Parnell Square North; tel: 01 872 2077; www.writersmuseum.com; Mon–Sat 10am–5pm, Sun, public hols 11am–5pm; admission charge; bus: 13, 16, 123; map p.132 B3

No visitor to Dublin can escape its literary heritage, be it commemo-

Right and below: a Bernard Shaw exhibition at the Original Print Gallery.

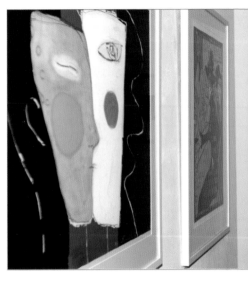

rated in a statue, displayed on the wall in a pub, or recognised in a museum. The Dublin Writers Museum is a shrine to all those literary figures and is housed in a beautiful 18th-century mansion. From the early days of dramatist George Farquhar and the wit and poet Jonathan Swift, through to the Victorian/Edwardian days of the infamous Oscar Wilde, and on to Yeats, Shaw, Joyce, Beckett and Behan, Dublin wins the literary prize. The emphasis is not just on the literary figures of the past but also on contemporary writers and the international literary scene. Paintings, photographs and memorabilia add a visual dimension to the written word.

SEE ALSO LITERATURE, P.76

GAA Museum

New Stand, Croke Park, St Joseph's Avenue; tel: 01 819 2323; www.museum.gaa.ie; daily 9.30am–5pm, July–Aug until 6pm, not open on match days; admission charge; bus: 3, 11, 16

The Gaelic Athletic Association is Ireland's largest sporting and cultural organisation. The museum is dedicated to Ireland's national games – hurling, Gaelic football, camogie (hurling for women) and handball. This is not just about the sports but about the cultural heritage behind them

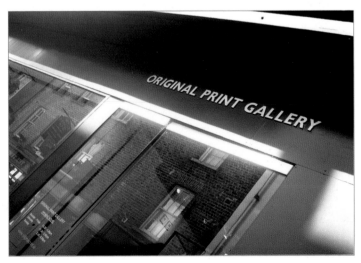

and the intensity of their following. There are daily tours of the stadium giving a behind-the-scenes peep into this national obsession.
SEE ALSO SPORTS, P.112

James Joyce Centre

35 North Great George's Street; tel: 01 878 8547; www.jamesjoyce.ie; Tue–Sat 10am–5pm, Sun noon–5pm; admission charge; bus: 40a; map p.132 C3
Visitors from around the world come to pay homage to Dublin's great literary genius, James Joyce. All you could ever want to know about the great man and his works is to be found here. You can join a walking tour to visit the haunts of Joyce and the hero of his work *Ulysses*, Leopold Bloom. If you visit the city on 16 June, Dublin is transformed for the Bloomsday celebrations. The centre not only concentrates on Joyce's time in Dublin but also on Paris, where he spent much of his creative life.
SEE ALSO FESTIVALS AND EVENTS, P.55; LITERATURE, P.76

BALLSBRIDGE AND AROUND
National Print Museum

Garrison Chapel, Beggar's Bush, Haddington Road; tel: 01 660 3770; www.nationalprint musem.ie; Mon–Fri 9am–5pm, Sat–Sun 2pm–5pm; admission charge; bus: 7, 45, 63
This idiosyncratic museum was set up in 1996 in a former soldiers' chapel to document and display the history of printing in Ireland. It endeavours to save and protect machinery used in the production of the written word in an age when digital printing is rapidly taking over. There are some wonderful examples of hand-printing presses and of early mechanical printing machines. Guided tours, lectures, workshops and special events all help to keep the spirit of printing alive.

There are several small print studios in Dublin, particularly in the Temple Bar area. The **Original Print Gallery** (4 Temple Bar; tel: 01 677 3657; www.originalprint.ie; Tue–Fri 10.30am–5.30pm, Sat 11am–5pm, Sun 2pm–6pm; free; bus: 66a, 66b, 67a; map p.136 B1) specialises in contemporary prints and showcases the best of Irish and international printmaking. All prints are handmade, using skilful practices. The **Black Church Print Studio** (tel: 01 677 3629; www.print.ie) is based above the Original Print Gallery and provides space for up to 200 artists a year creating prints and attending workshops. The **Graphic Studio Gallery** (Temple Bar (through arch off Cope Street); tel: 01 679 8021; www.graphicstudio dublin.com; Mon–Fri 10am–5.30pm, Sat 11am–5pm; free; bus: 66a, 66b, 67a; map p.136 B1) is another impressive print gallery promoting Irish and international artists.

Music

Dublin is renowned as one of the most musical cities in the world; the chances are you will hear music wherever you go, and the locals don't need an excuse to break into song. The style of music runs across all genres, from classical, jazz and traditional Irish to rock and pop, and the venues are varied, too, encompassing acoustics equal to the best. A wide spectrum of annual festivals celebrates music in a big way *(see Festivals and Events, p.54)*. Pick up the free *Event Guide (see Essentials, p.52)* to keep up with what's happening. For more live music venues see *Bars and Cafés, p.32,* and *Nightlife, p.94.*

CLASSICAL MUSIC

In an otherwise vibrant musical city, Dublin's classical music and opera scene keeps a fairly low profile. Strange, since this is a city accredited with hosting the first performance of Handel's *Messiah*, in 1742 (which is reprised each Easter at Fishamble Street opposite Christ Church Cathedral, *see p.42*). There are very few renowned Irish classical performers or composers, and productions can be limited; call the box office at the appropriate venue about forthcoming events or check the listings in the *Irish Times*.

There are two resident orchestras, however, the **Dublin Philharmonic Orchestra** and **RTÉ National Symphony Orchestra**, while **Opera Ireland** takes the stage at the Gaiety Theatre on a seasonal basis. Occasionally classical concerts are also staged at non-music-specific venues such as Dublin Castle, St Patrick's

Above: in performance at the National Concert Hall.

Cathedral or the Hugh Lane Gallery.

VENUES

Gaiety Theatre

South King Street; tel: 01 677 1717; www.gaietytheatre.com; box office: Mon–Sat 10am–6pm (or performance start time); bus: 92, 118, 746; map p.136 B3
Among a varied programme of events, this traditional Victorian theatre, complete with red velvet curtains and boxes, plays host to Dublin's most prolific opera company, Opera Ireland. Performances only take place four times a year and tickets sell out fast, so reserve well in advance.

National Concert Hall

Earlsfort Terrace; tel: 01 417 000; www.nch.ie; box office: Mon–Sat 10am–7pm (and two hours before performances); bus: 14a, 15a, 128; map p.136 C1
Built for the International Exhibition of Arts and Manufacturers in 1865, this building has a splendid Georgian facade and is Dublin's largest classical music hall. It stages a rich and varied schedule throughout the year, including weekly performances given by the resident orchestra, the RTÉ National Symphony Orchestra. A redevelopment plan due to start 2010 and finish in 2013 will turn the venue into a

Left: traditional Irish music...
and a few pints.

Traditional Irish music is one of
the reasons so many tourists
flock to Dublin, hoping to catch
an exhilarating traditional music
session in one of the many
pubs *(see Traditional Pubs,
p.118)*. If time is short, a great
way to experience the best
spots is to take the **Traditional
Irish Musical Pub Crawl** *(see
Walks, Bus Tours and Boat
Trips, p.126)*. For more on traditional Irish music see *Celtic
Roots and Culture, p.39*.

VENUES

Bleu Note Bar & Club
61–62 Capel Street;
tel: 01 878 3371;
www.bleunote.ie; daily
8.30pm–11.30pm, Fri–Sat
until 2.30am; bus: 37, 39a, 70a;
map p.132 A1
On Friday and Saturdays,
low lighting in the
basement creates a
soulful atmosphere in
which to listen to live jazz,
while upstairs blues, funk,
soul and swing rotate on
other nights.

world-class performance
space – the National Con-
cert Hall will continue to
function almost as normal
during this period.

CONTEMPORARY MUSIC

When it comes to modern
music, this city is responsible for some of the
biggest megastars to
climb the record charts.
Phil Lynott and his band
Thin Lizzy were probably
the first international rock
success story to come out
of Dublin, and other pro-
lific pop and rock artists
who have followed in their
footsteps include
Westlife, **Ronan Keating**,
Sir Bob Geldolf's band
The Boomtown Rats and
Sinéad O'Connor. But it
is **Bono** and **U2** that have
achieved an almost saintly
status in the eyes of most
Dubliners. Dublin's **Rock-
'n'Roll, Writers Bus Tour**
*(see Walks, Bus Tours and
Boat Trips, p.127)* gives an
insight into where these
superstars worked, lived
and played before they

made it big. Dublin is
included on most major
international stars' tour
circuit, particularly since
the newly revamped O2
arena opened. If you're
not in pursuit of headlin-
ers, you don't need to go
far in this city to come
across a venue with live
music of some sort or
another, whether it's jazz,
rock or pop.

Below: Bono of U2, Dublin's most famous musical export.

Left: a street performer plays his whistle for the crowds.

house at the back. Still family owned, it's now dedicated to live jazz and blues. Many a musician has got their first break here and top musicians return again and again.

The O2
North Wall Quay; tel: 01 819 8888; www.theo2.ie; hours vary with concerts; bus: 53a, 151, shuttle bus from St Stephen's Green, Eden Quay and Connolly Station every 20 minutes from 6pm, Luas: The Point
Reopened in 2008 after a major revamp, the former Point can now supply the very best in sound and has the capacity for over 24,000 screaming fans, who flock here to see their idols perform on the international rock and pop circuit.

Vicar Street
58–59 Thomas Street; tel: 01 454 5533; hours vary with gigs; bus: 51b, 78a, 123; map p.135 E3
This well-respected, medium-sized venue is well laid out and has a top-notch PA and lighting system. The roll call of acts that have appeared here is testament to its quality.

MUSIC SHOPS
Celtic Note
14–15 Nassau Street; tel: 01 670 4157; www.celticnote.com; Mon–Sat 9.30am–6.30pm, Sun 11am–6pm; bus: 10a, 13a, 15a; map p.137 D3
Music enthusiasts come to

Button Factory
Curved Street; tel: 01 670 9202; http://ww2.buttonfac tory.ie; hours vary with event; bus: 50, 66a, 66b; map p.136 A1
Reopened in 2007 with a new layout, bigger capacity and state-of-the-art equipment, this is now one of the city's most exciting places to enjoy live music.

Crawdaddy
Old Harcourt Station, Harcourt Street; tel: 01 476 3374; www.pod.ie; hours vary with event; bus: 48a; map p.136 B1
Custom-built in two tiers for the purpose of live gigs, Crawdaddy has established itself as one of Dublin's leading live music venues since opening in 2004. An eclectic mix of artists rock the house here, encompassing the best in indie, dance, rock, electro, folk, funk, hip-hop, reggae, world and soul.

Helix
Dublin City University, Glasnevin; tel: 01 700 7000; www.thehelix.ie; box office: Mon–Sat 10am–6pm, performance days until 8pm; bus: 3, 13, 16
This stunning building of glass and granite offers two very different spaces for a variety of live music. **Mahony Hall** seats over 1,260 and has been designed for acoustic excellence, while **The Space** is smaller and suits jazz and blues sessions.

JJ Smyth's
12 Aungier Street; tel: 01 475 2565; www.jjsmyths,com; Mon–Thur 10.30am–11.30pm, Fri–Sat 10.30am–12.30am, Sun 12.30pm–11pm; bus: 16a, 19a, 83; map p.136 B2
Poet Thomas Moore was born in this building, which started out in the 1730s as a grocery with a pubic

Right: Dublin is often a stop on major acts' tours.

this small, dedicated Irish music shop in search of a particular folk or ballad album.

Charles Byrne

21–22 Stephen Street Lower; tel: 01 478 1773; www.charles byrnemusic.ie; Tue–Fri 9am–5.30pm, Sat 9.30am–5pm; bus: 16a, 19a, 83; map p.136 B3

Founded in 1870, the handmade *bodhráns* (goat-skin drums) displayed at this family-owned instrument shop are fascinating to see, even if traditional music is not your thing. Knowledgeable staff can tell you everything there is to know about stringed instruments, too.

The city streets of Dublin are often alive with talented – some not so talented – street musicians from all walks of life, playing a wide range of instruments and performing anything from rock and classical to Irish jigs. Grafton Street and St Stephen's Green are the usual spots to discover more sedate options, while in Temple Bar lively crowds gather around and add to the fun with impromptu dancing.

Claddagh Records

2 Cecilia Street; tel: 01 677 0262; www.claddaghrecords. com; Mon–Fri 10.30am–5.30pm, Sat noon–5.20pm; bus: 50, 66a, 66b; map p.136 A1

Claddagh Records claim to hold the largest collection of traditional Irish music in Ireland, and if you can't find the recording you're looking for, the helpful staff are willing to try to track it down.

Waltons

2–5 Frederick Street North; tel: 01 874 7805; www.waltons.ie; Mon–Sat 9am–6pm, Sun noon–5pm; bus: 3, 10, 16; map p.132 B3

A musical emporium stacked high with new and second-hand instruments, and a huge range of CDs, music books, sheet music and other must-have accessories.

Nightlife

Some visitors arrive in the city with no intention of ever seeing daylight; for them, Dublin is all about the nightlife. The long-standing stag and hen party trend is on its way out though, and the recent increase in sophisticated bars and 'super pubs' is making nightclubs scarcer here, although a decent number remain. Meanwhile, the Irish are celebrated for their wit and an ability to laugh at themselves, and Dublin's dynamic comedy scene is evidence of this, breeding Irish comedy stars such as Dave Allen and Ardal O'Hanlon. For further nightlife see *Bars and Cafés, p.32, Music, p.90, Gay and Lesbian, p.62,* and *Traditional Pubs, p.118.*

CASINOS
Club Oasis Casino
4 Westmoreland Street; tel: 01 474 3273; www.amusementcity.com; daily 3pm–1am; bus: 46a, 150, 746; map p.132 C1
With over 250 slots and 13 tables (including blackjack, roulette and poker), this is Dublin's biggest gaming establishment, based here in the very centre of the city since 1974.

Silks Club Casino
24 Earlsfort Terrace; tel: 01 475 9191; www.silksclub.ie; Tue–Sun 8pm–6am; bus: 14a, 15a, 128; map p.137 C1
This sophisticated gaming club is not out of place in the exclusive area near St Stephen's Green. Free membership is available on entry with a driver's licence or passport. Attentive staff look after the guests while they try their hand at blackjack or roulette.

CLUBS AND DISCOS
Club M
Cope Street; tel: 01 671 5274; www.clubm.ie; daily 10pm–3am; bus: 46a, 150, 746; map p.136 B1
This multilevel nightclub with galleries overlooking the main dance floor has been the focus of nightlife in Temple Bar for over a decade, and is still busy seven nights a week with a dancing crowd who lose themselves in the energising vibes.

Lillie's Bordello
Adam Court, Grafton Street; tel: 01 679 9204; www.lilliesbordello.ie; daily 11pm–2.30am; bus: 10a, 14a, 70b; map p.136 C3
Just off fashionable Grafton Street, this prestigious nightclub is the place to go for an evening of celebrity-spotting. The decor is nothing special and drinks are very expensive, but the club's reputation keeps pulling in an Armani-clad, champagne-drinking clientele.

Left: DJ Carl Cox mixes it up at a party in Dublin.

edy Club is found at the Ha'penny Bridge Inn in Temple Bar on Wednesday and Sunday nights; **Comedy Dublin** is at the Belvedere Bar, Great Denmark Street, on Sunday evening and at Sheehan's Pub, Chatham Street, on Tuesday evening; while the **International Comedy Club** operates at the International Bar, Wicklow Street, Thursday to Sunday.

Laughter Lounge
Basement 4, 8 Eden Quay; tel: 01 878 3003; www.laughter lounge.ie; Thur–Sat 7pm–11.30pm; bus: 15a, 128, 142; map p.133 C1
Ireland's premier, purpose-built comedy club, which hosts some of the world's favourite stand-up comedians, will guarantee an evening full of laughter. Shows start at 8pm in the spacious auditorium.

Left: Dublin retains a reputation for having a big nightlife scene: perfect for hardcore clubbers.

The Vaults
Harbourmaster Place, IFSC; tel: 01 605 4700; www.thevaults.ie; Mon–Sat noon–11.30pm, nightclub Fri, Sat 10pm–2.30am; bus: 53, 151, DART: Connolly, Luas: George's Dock, map p.133 D2
One of Dublin's hottest nightspots is housed in a transformed vault, which reveals a dramatic cave-like setting for some of the best international DJs to spin their decks while serious dancers take to the floor.

Viper Room
5 Aston Quay; tel: 01 672 5566; Tue–Sun 8pm–4am; bus: 78a, 90, 92; map p.132 C1
A late-night lounge bar decked out in red and purple, the Viper Room can be a bit of a slow starter. But by around 10pm it gradually fills up and by midnight live music upstairs and a pulsating disco down get things going.

COMEDY CLUBS
Several comedy clubs have arrived on the scene, taking up residency in venues around the city where they stage top-rate comedians and open-mike nights. Com-

As Dublin is fairly compact, walking back at night is not too much hassle, and normally there are plenty of bodies around (not necessarily always upright). But if you would prefer to avoid the normally harmless party revellers, call a taxi; note you will pay a premium. With so many people trying to get back late at night, taxis can be in short supply, so to be sure of getting one book a return trip before you go out. Buses stop at 11.30pm, but a limited Nitelink service operates Thur–Sat until 4.30am. The DART stops at 11.30pm and the Luas at 12.30am.

Right: a hedonistic dancer.

Parks and Gardens

Dubliners have every right to be proud of their city parks and gardens, which are some of the best in Europe. Despite Dublin being a compact, congested and busy city, you will discover a park or garden in the most unlikely of places. From the vast Phoenix Park, the largest urban park in Europe, to the pretty, small Georgian squares, you are never far from an open green space and a chance to relax from city life. In summer, locals lunch in the parks and gardens, occasionally to the sounds of concerts, jazz or brass bands.

FAR WEST AND PHOENIX PARK

Irish National War Memorial Park

South Circular Road, Islandbridge; tel: 01 475 7816; www.heritageireland.ie; Mon–Fri 8.30am–dusk, Sat–Sun 10am–dusk; free; bus: 51, 68, 69

These tranquil gardens were designed by architect Sir Edwin Lutyens to commemorate the 49,000 Irish soldiers who died in World War I. The name of every soldier is recorded in the beautiful, illustrated manuscripts by Harry Clarke found in the granite 'bookrooms' in the gardens.

Phoenix Park

Phoenix Park; tel: 01 677 0095; www.heritageireland.ie; daily 24 hours, Visitor Centre: daily 10am–5pm; free; bus: 10, 25, 26, Luas: Heuston Station then shuttle bus daily 7am–6pm (starts 10am Sat and Sun), departs on the hour every hour; map p.130 A2

If you don't want to walk right through the park there is a shuttle bus run-

ning from Heuston Station to the informative Visitor Centre in the centre of the park. Next to the centre is the fully restored **Ashtown Castle**, a building discovered when the 18th-century mansion encasing it was demolished owing to dry rot. Within the confines of this vast park are **Dublin Zoo**, the American ambassador's home and the Irish president's residence, **Aras an Uachtaráin**.

For those looking for activity, in addition to walking and cycling trails, there are opportunities for running, hurling, polo, cricket and football. Look out for the herd of wild fallow deer and some fine monuments.

SEE ALSO CHILDREN, P.41

ST STEPHEN'S GREEN AND AROUND

Iveagh Gardens

Clonmel Street; tel: 01 475 7816; Mon–Sat 8am–6pm, Sun 10am–6pm, closes at dusk in winter; free; bus: 14a, 15a, 128; map p.136 C1

Blessington Street Basin is regarded as Dublin's secret garden, and offers a haven of peace for humans and local wildlife, 10 minutes' walk from Parnell Square. Just far enough off the beaten track to miss the crowds, the gardens were landscaped in the 1990s. Formerly a reservoir built as part of Dublin's water supply, it began to fall into disrepair in the 1970s and now its small lake with an inland island attracts ducks, swans and the occasional person.

These gardens, among the finest and least known of Dublin's green spaces, are hidden behind Iveagh House, which was donated to the State by Sir Robert Guinness in 1939. The gardens were designed by Ninian Niven in 1865, and blend the classical English landscape style with the French formal style, echoing the Bois de Boulogne in Paris. They include a rustic grotto and cascade, fountains, maze, rosar-

Left: Furry Glen is a protected wildlife area of Phoenix Park.

fail to please. There are several sculptures in the park, and the grand **Fusiliers' Arch** is located in the northwest corner.

SEE ALSO STATUES AND MONUMENTS, P.114

GEORGIAN DISTRICT AND MUSEUMS

Merrion Square Park

Merrion Square; tel: 01 222 5278; daily 10am–dusk; free; bus: 45; map p.137 D3

The park sits amid the most perfect of Georgian squares, one-time home to many illustrious Irish names, including Oscar Wilde. His wonderfully languid, life-like statue can be seen in the northwest corner of the park. The park's earliest plans date to the late 18th century, and it was designed to emulate an English garden, but its fashionable address didn't prevent it from being used as a soup kitchen during the famine. Within the park are several fine sculptures, a collection of old Dublin lamp posts, a central floral garden, a

ium, American garden, archery grounds and woodlands. A programme of restoration in 1995 and subsequent conservation have brought the gardens back to their original glory. This is the perfect place to escape the city on a warm summer's day.

St Stephen's Green

St Stephen's Green; tel: 01 475 7816; www.heritageireland.ie; Mon–Sat 7.30am–dusk, Sun and public hols 9.30am–dusk; free; bus: 92, 118, 746; map p.136 C2

The most loved and best known of Dublin's parks is a sanctuary for both office workers and visitors, and is especially popular during summer with its lunchtime concerts. It is a far cry from its original purpose of common land used for public hangings. Set so close to the busy shopping areas, the park's pleasant tree-lined walks, colourful borders and ornamental lake cannot

Below left: the *Children of Lír* statue *(see p.98)*. **Below right:** relaxing on St Stephen's Green.

Top: walking in Merrion Square Park.
Above: a glasshouse at the National Botanic Gardens.

dens.ie; mid-Feb to mid-Nov daily 9am–6pm, mid-Nov to mid-Feb 9am–4.30pm, glasshouses/alpines restricted; free; bus: 13, 19, 40, train: Drumcondra

The gardens include an arboretum, rock garden, sensory garden and a fine annual display of colourful plants. Of particular interest are the superb examples of 19th-century curvilinear glasshouses. Notable specimens housed within include the rare and unusually named handkerchief tree (so called because the whitish leaves enclosing each flower resemble handkerchiefs), which comes from China. There is an informative Visitor Centre and there are free guided tours of the gardens every Sunday at noon and 2.30pm.

O'CONNELL STREET AND BEYOND

Garden of Remembrance

Parnell Square East; tel: 01 821 3021; Apr–Sept daily 8.30am–6pm, Oct–Nov 9.30am–4pm; free; bus: 1, 2, 14a; map p.132 B3

These gardens, created in 1966, are a poignant reminder of the deaths that occurred during the Easter Rising of 1916 and a place of quiet reflection. When the rising was quashed, those that survived were marched to this spot and held in the gardens overnight before being transported to their fate in Kilmainham Gaol. The focal point of the gardens is the commemorative statue *The Children of Lír* by Oisín Kelly.

SEE ALSO MUSEUMS AND GALLERIES, P.79; STATUES AND MONUMENTS, P.114

heather garden and a playground. Local artists display their works on the railings at weekends.

SEE ALSO STATUES AND MONUMENTS, P.114

NORTH OF THE LIFFEY, WEST

Glasnevin Cemetery

Finglas Road, Glasnevin; tel: 01 830 1133; www.glasnevin-cemetery.ie; Mon–Sat 8.30am–4.30pm, Sun 9am–4.30pm; free; bus: 13, 19, 40, train: Drumcondra

At this vast and atmospheric cemetery, three different guided tours reveal the graves of many famous Irish men and women, including freedom fighters Michael Collins, Eamon de Valera and Countess Marciewicz, playwright Brendan Behan and novelist Christy Brown. For some the paupers' graves are the most poignant, a reminder of the devastation wrought by famine and cholera in the 1840s.

National Botanic Gardens, Glasnevin

Glasnevin Hill Road; tel: 01 804 0300; www.botanicgar-

Mountjoy Park

Mountjoy Square; tel: 01 222 5278; daily 10am–dusk; free; bus: 46B, 46C, 63; map p.133 C4

Mountjoy Park occupies 1.8 hectares (4½ acres) at the centre of what was once considered one of Dublin's premier Georgian squares before it was neglected and became run-down. Now spruced up, the park boasts a five-a-side football pitch, tennis courts, playground and attractive floral displays.

BALLSBRIDGE AND AROUND
Herbert Park

Ballsbridge; tel: 01 222 5278; daily 10am–dusk; free; bus: 5, 7, 45

Although not large at 13 hectares (32 acres), this park is full of amenities for locals and visitors alike and features sports fields and tennis courts.

There is a children's play area, a bowling green and facilities for croquet and boules. The pond, constructed in 1907, is full of breeding carp and is fre-

Out in Dublin's northeastern suburbs is the lovely **St Anne's Park** *(see picture, below)* with its world-renowned rose gardens. An excellent park for its recreational facilities, extensive woods and walled gardens, a visit between June and September will see the magnificent roses in full bloom.

quented by ducks and other water birds. Add to this floral displays, walking trails and occasional band performances, and the picture is complete.

Restaurants

The past decade has seen Dublin's restaurant scene become increasingly cosmopolitan, offering cuisines from all over the world. Talented young chefs have reinvented menus, putting greater emphasis on quality local ingredients. Eating out can be expensive here, though, and it pays to take advantage of fixed-price and 'early bird' menus. Around St Stephen's Green are many top-class restaurants that could challenge anybody's credit card. For less expensive options stay near Temple Bar, and there are increasingly more good-value places moving in around Grand Canal Square. See also *Bars and Cafés, p.32.*

FAR WEST AND PHOENIX PARK
Hole in the Wall
12 Blackhorse Avenue; tel: 01 838 9491; www.holeinthewall dublin.com; €; dining room Wed–Sat 5–10pm, Sun 12.30–9pm; bus: 10, 25, 26, Luas: Heuston

Named after a practice that once existed of serving drinks through a hole in the wall to Phoenix Park, this local treasure has come a long way from the beef and Guinness pie of old. The McCaffery family proudly use Irish-only suppliers of quality fresh produce, and even the chips are cooked with duck fat.

SOUTH OF THE LIFFEY, WEST
Chez Max
1 Palace Street; tel: 01 633 7215; www.chezmax.ie; €€; Mon–Fri 8am–11pm, Sat, Sun 11am–midnight; bus 50, 56a, 123; map p.136 B4

It's easy to imagine you are really in 1940s Paris at this adorable French bistro, which opens out onto a cobbled street in front of Dublin Castle. As you would expect, the food is totally Parisian; dishes such as frog's legs for starters followed by *boeuf bourguignon*, cooked to perfection.

Darwins
16 Aungier Street; tel: 01 475 7511; www.darwins.ie; Mon–Sat 5.30–11pm, Wed–Fri noon–3pm; €€; bus: 16a, 19a, 83; map p.136 B3

As expected from a restaurant owned by a butcher, the steaks here are sublime. The fresh meat comes direct from his shop, which is reflected in the beautifully cooked

Prices for an average two-course meal for one with a glass of wine:	
€€€	over €45
€€	€28–45
€	under €28

Left: mouth-watering specials and friendly staff.

Left: the Tea Room at The Clarence *(see p.102)*.

15a; map p.136 B4

For a thoroughly enjoyable culinary experience, visit this basement restaurant where adventurous, satisfying Lebanese food is served in an exotic Arabic setting. If you are hungry enough, go all out and have the traditional meze. Spicy Lebanese wines complement the meal.

Cornucopia

19 Wicklow Street; tel: 01 677 7583; www.cornucopia.ie; €; Mon–Sat 8.30am–9pm, Sat until 8pm, Sun noon–7pm; bus: 10a, 14a, 70b; map p.136 C4

This successful vegetarian restaurant began life as a health food shop in 1986. So successful, there are plans in place to expand into the building next door retaining the signature red frontage and, most importantly, the amazing selection of freshly prepared healthy dishes.

Above: delicious Irish bread.

and presented dishes. Surprisingly enough, vegetarians are catered for, too. Genuine, friendly service will make sure you are totally sold on the place, if you weren't already.

Lord Edward

23 Christchurch Place; tel: 01 454 2420; www.lordedward.ie; €€; Mon–Fri 12.30–2.30pm, 6–10.45pm, Sat 6–10.45pm; bus: 50, 56a, 123; map p.136 A4

On the second floor of a historic tavern you'll find the oldest seafood restaurant in Dublin, established in 1890. There is much to choose from, prepared in a simple, unpretentious way that is second to none. The delightful, old-fashioned atmosphere is backed up by courteous old-fashioned service.

CENTRAL CORE, SOUTH OF THE LIFFEY
Il Baccaro

Diceman's Corner; tel: 01 671 4597; www.ilbaccaro.com; €€; Mon–Thur 6.30–11pm, Fri–Sun noon–11pm; bus: 50, 66a, 66b; map p.132 A1

You can easily overlook this rustic Italian *osteria* tucked away in the corner of the square. Steps lead down into an intimate 17th-century vaulted wine cellar with stone arches opening out into additional dining space. Expect to dine on consistently good authentic Italian fare, while the wine comes straight from the barrel.

The Cedar Tree

11 St Andrew's Street; tel: 01 677 2121; €; daily 5.30–11.30pm; bus: 10a, 13a,

In the midst of Dublin's growing reputation as a significant player among the world's culinary metropolises have come several celebrity chefs looking for a home for their next venture. Some to watch out for are Kevin Thornton, who delivers his culinary skills at the **Fitzwilliam Hotel** *(see Hotels, p.69)*; Patrick Guilbaud, who has been delighting diners since 1981 at the **Merrion Hotel** *(see Hotels, p.69)*; the owner of **L'Ecrivain** (www.lecrivain.com), Derry Clarke; and Richard Corrigan, who has gained great critical acclaim at **Bentleys Oyster Bar & Grill** (www.bentleys dublin.com).

Eating in the Tea Room at **The Clarence** (*see Hotels, p.67*) is a real dining treat, and, contrary to belief, it won't cost you the earth. Fighting back against the economic downturn, the Tea Room is currently offering special menu options that are superb value. The 'Market Dinner Menu' offers two courses for €24 and three for €26, including homemade bread, tea or coffee and homemade chocolates.

Eden
Meeting House Square; tel: 01 670 5372; www.edenrestaurant.ie; €€; daily 12.30–3pm, 6–10.30pm, Sun until 10pm; bus: 50, 66a, 66b; map p.136 A1

A veteran of Temple Bar, Eden has retained its popularity, although it is starting to look a little frayed around the edges. The two-storey dining space has a large outdoor terrace that overflows onto Meeting House Square, enabling diners to absorb the atmosphere of Temple Bar while munching on contemporary dishes with a distinctive Irish flavour.

Les Frères Jacques
74 Dame Street; tel: 01 679 4555; www.lesfreresjacques.com; €€€; Mon–Fri 12.30–2.20pm, 7.30–10.30pm, Sat 7.15–11pm; bus: 50, 56a, 123; map p.136 B1

This is one of Dubin's best-loved restaurants, and it's easy to see why.

Prices for an average two-course meal for one with a glass of wine:
€€€   over €45
€€   €28–45
€   under €28

Everything from the French cuisine and stylish setting to the warm French staff is straight out of the top drawer. But quality doesn't come cheap, so you might want to save this one for a special occasion.

Gallagher's Boxty House
20–21 Temple Bar; tel: 01 677 2762; www.boxtyhouse.ie; €–€€; daily noon–11.30pm; bus: 50, 66a, 66b; map p.136 B1

Apart from the house speciality dish, the boxty (*Arán Boct Tí*; a pancake cooked on a griddle served with a choice of filling, originally just potato), the unique brown-bread ice cream, good-humoured waiters and a country kitchen atmosphere all contribute to making this a tourist honey pot. Live music is performed Mon–Fri 4pm–6pm.

Monty's of Kathmandu
28 Eustace Street; tel: 01 670 4911; www.montys.ie; €€; daily 5.30–11pm; bus: 50, 66a, 66b; map p.136 A1

Monty's excellent reputation for award-winning authentic Nepalese food and Eastern charm extends far and wide. Don't be put off if you've never eaten Nepalese before, the staff here are more than willing to give advice on their intriguing dishes, which are made using secret ingredients to produce a special exotic taste.

Saba
26–28 Clarendon Street; tel: 01 679 2000; www.sabadublin.com; €; daily noon–late; bus: 16a, 19a, 54a; map p.136 B3

Saba remains true to its Thai and Vietnamese heritage, with the focus on fresh, healthy ingredients and a passion for recognisable, intense flavours. Polished concrete floors, black wood and leather contrast with vibrant colours to give Saba its own trendy identity.

Shebeen Chic
4 South Great George's Street; tel: 01 679 9667; www.shebeenchic.ie; €–€€; daily noon–5pm, 5.30–10pm (Thur–Sat until 11pm); bus:

Left: at Il Primo is a favourite for rustic Italian fare.

Tue–Fri 12.30–2pm, 6–11pm, Sat 6–11pm; bus: 11, 78, 118; map p.137 D1

Awarded best newcomer by the Restaurant Association of Ireland in 2006; food connoisseurs are still flooding to this understated dining room with sophisticated touches of elegance. Cooking is a mix of rustic French with exciting twists using the finest ingredients, and the largely French wine list is excellent, too.

Peploe's

16 St Stephen's Green North; tel: 01 676 3144; www.peploes.com; €€; daily noon–midnight; bus: 92, 118, 746; map p.137 C2

Always buzzing and full of life, particularly at lunchtime, when it attracts a cosmopolitan business crowd, this cellar restaurant has a warm, chatty atmosphere. Oak panelling, murals and leather upholstery furnish the dining room with a smart bistro look where perfectly cooked, often quite unusual, modern European dishes are served.

Il Primo

16 Montague Street; tel: 01 478 3373; www.ilprimo.ie; €€; Mon–Fri 12.30–10pm, Sat 12.30–11pm; bus: 48a; map p.136 B2

Il Primo has been housed in this cosy period house for over a decade. Under new ownership since 2007, it has been spruced up while still exuding old-fashioned, simple Italian warmth. The food remains rustic Italian but with an

16a, 19a, 83; map p.136 B3

This quirky concept has certainly got people talking. It is decked out with battered, recycled items such as black toilet seats on the wall and shabby mismatched furniture, but the rich, earthy traditional Irish food is

certainly not downbeat, produced by an Irish chef who once worked under the renowned Kevin Thornton.

ST STEPHEN'S GREEN AND AROUND
Bang Café

Merrion Row; tel: 01 676 0898; www.bangrestaurant.com; €€; Mon–Sat 12.30–3pm, 6–11pm; bus: 10a; map p.137 D2

Two brothers from Denmark own Bang Café and have stamped their personality on the pristine, minimalist interior, the perfect background for innovative Irish cooking at the highest level, using locally sourced fresh organic produce.

Dax

23 Pembroke Street Upper; tel: 01 676 1494; www.dax.ie; €€;

Left: live music over dinner at Gallagher's Boxty House.

103

Right: One Pico's smart dining room.

unexpected twist, and the Tuscan wines now include new exciting examples sourced by the owners while in Italy.

Seagrass
30 South Richmond Street, Portobello; tel: 01 478 9595; www.seagrassdublin.com; €; Tue–Sat noon–2.30pm, 5.30–10pm, Sun noon–4pm, 5.30–10pm; bus: 14a, 15a, 74a
Simple, well-made modern European food using good fresh produce is the concept here, and Seagrass hits the mark. The smart frontage draws you to this relatively new restaurant, and fresh, clean lines continue inside with bright aquamarine tones. You can choose to eat in the main dining room, secluded basement or outside on the terrace in warm weather.

GEORGIAN DISTRICT AND MUSEUMS
Balzac
La Stampa Hotel, 35 Dawson Street; tel: 01 677 8611; www.lastampa.ie; €€; Mon–Sat 6–11pm, Fri also 12.30–3pm; bus: 10a, 128, 746; map p.137 C3
Take the opportunity to dress up at this hotel restaurant that probably has the most exquisite dining room in Dublin. Flowing sheer drapes, marble pillars and a beautiful ceiling inset with

Prices for an average two-course meal for one with a glass of wine:
€€€ over €45
€€ €28–45
€ under €28

stained glass set a scene that is every bit as refined as the consistently good French cooking.

The Farm
3 Dawson Street; tel: 01 671 8654; €; daily 11am–11pm; bus: 10a, 128, 746; map p.137 C3
The Farm brings an affordable organic theme to Dublin that concentrates on home-style favourites such as burgers, roast chicken and pastas, but with an additional tasty edge. The jazzy, white interior with lime-green seating is always busy, but pavement tables add extra space on a sunny day.

Fire
Mansion House, Dawson Street; tel: 01 676 7200; www.mansionhouse.ie/fire;

€€–€€€; Mon–Wed 5.30–10pm, Thur–Sat noon–3pm, 5.30–10pm; bus: 10a, 128, 746; map p.137 C3
Sip a cocktail on the illuminated terrace before you dine inside what is part of the Lord Mayor's residence. High vaulted ceilings and stained-glass windows enclose a large space that has a real wow factor, using flame-red and a wood-fired oven to accentuate the theme. Food is a mixture of the contemporary and traditionally rustic European.

One Pico
5–6 Molesworth Place, School House Lane; tel: 01 676 0300; www.onepico.com; €€; Mon–Sat 12.15–2.30pm, 6–11pm; bus: 10a, 128, 746;

Right: the modern Bridge Bar & Grill.

map p.137 C3
Talented chef and owner, Eamonn O'Reilly is legendary for exceptional cooking executed in his own unique style, so much so, he now owns two other restaurants in Dublin: **Pacific** and **Bleu Bistro**, both on Dame Street. Only first-class ingredients go into his classic-French-with-an-Irish-twist dishes, and the menu changes monthly. An extensive wine list does justice to the meal.

Pearl Brasserie
20 Merrion Street Upper; tel: 01 661 3572; www.pearl-brasserie.com; €€€; Mon–Fri noon–2.30, 6–10.30pm, Sat 6–10.30pm; bus: 10a, 45; map p.137 D2
Intimate alcoves, tropical fish aquariums, soft music playing and the smell of an open fire all go towards creating the soothing environment at this very sleek restaurant. Add to that

Sébastien Masi's assured French cooking and you have the recipe for a delightful meal.

The Pig's Ear
4 Nassau Street; tel: 01 670 3865; www.thepigsear.ie; €; Mon–Sat 9am–10pm; bus: 10a, 13a, 15a; map p.137 D3
Upstairs overlooking the grounds of Trinity College, the dining room is quite plain with varnished floorboards and dark-wood furniture, while a few ornamental pigs add a splash of humour. Honest Irish favourites such as shepherd's pie appear on the menu, cooked and presented in a more adventurous way.

DOCKLANDS AND CANALS
Bridge Bar & Grill
The Malting Tower, Grand Canal Quay; tel: 01 639 0032; www.bridgebarandgrill.ie; €; Mon–Sat 12.30–3.30pm, 6–11pm; DART: Grand Canal

Welcome aboard Dublin's floating restaurant! Moored alongside the quay in the resurgent Docklands area, former training vessel MV *Cill Airne* (www.mvcillairne.com) has brought an intriguing new dining experience to the city. You can eat in the shipshape **Quay 16** restaurant or in the less formal **Blue River Bistro** (Quay 16, North Wall Quay; tel: 01 817 8760; www.mvcill airne.com; Quay 16: Mon–Fri noon–3pm, 6pm–10pm, Sat 6pm–10pm; Bistro: daily noon–midnight; €–€€€; bus: 53a, 151, Luas: Mayor Square). The upper deck serves as an outdoor seating area that gives unrivalled views of the waterfront.

Dock
As the name suggests, this modern brasserie is tucked away under the DART railway bridge, which provides the odd tunnel-shaped dining area that, with the use of ele-

gant table settings and stylish seating, the owners have utilised perfectly. The simple but flawlessly executed food is big on flavour but not on price.

ely hq
Hanover Quay; tel: 01 633 9986; www.elywinebar.ie; €; Mon–Thur noon–11.30pm, Fri noon–12.30am, Sat 1pm–12.30am; bus: 2, 3, 77
Opened in 2007, the clean-cut lines here echo the urban surroundings of the developing south Docklands area. Diners join a young crowd munching on organic food accompanied by a glass of wine from ely's remarkable list, while enjoying the view over Grand Canal Square through large picture windows.

Il Fornaio: IFSC
1b Valentia House, Custom House Square; tel: 01 672 1853; www.ilfornaio.ie; €; Mon–Fri

9am–10pm, Sun 11am–9pm; bus: 53a, 151, Luas: Mayor Square; map p.133 D2
This welcome addition to the developing Docklands area offers no frills, just simple authentic Italian fare served with a cheery Italian smile. It's very small inside, but in good weather there are additional tables out on the pavement.

NORTH OF THE LIFFEY, WEST
Chapter One
18–19 Parnell Square North; tel: 01 873 2266; www.chap teronerestaurant.com; €€€; Tue–Fri 12.30–2pm, Sat 12.30–2pm, 6–11pm; bus: 13, 16, 123; map p.132 B3
In a basement beneath the Dublin Writers Museum, Chapter One's French-influenced, consistently top-notch, Irish cooking is considered to be the best north of the river, and the vaulted wine

Prices for an average two-course meal for one with a glass of wine:
€€€ over €45
€€ €28–45
€ under €28

cellar impresses, too. The pre-theatre menu is very popular.

Gallery Restaurant at the Church
Mary Street; tel: 01 828 0102; www.thechurch.ie; €€; daily 5–10pm; bus: 37, 39a, 70a, Luas: Jervis; map p.132 B1
The international food with an Irish flavour is fine, but most people come here to marvel at the aesthetics, as a stunning organ and huge stained-glass windows loom over the handsome restaurant and bustling café and bar down below.

101 Talbot
100–102 Talbot Street; tel: 01

Below: enjoy some excellent Irish cooking at Chapter One.

Above: quiches made with local ingredients.

874 5011; www.101talbot.com; €–€€; Tue–Sat 5–11pm; bus: 16a, 747; map p.133 C2
A great local favourite, albeit not in the most salubrious area, but that's soon forgotten once you enter the dining room and are greeted by the vivacious staff who serve flavoursome modern Irish dishes with Mediterranean and Middle Eastern influences.

BALLSBRIDGE AND AROUND

Lobster Pot
9 Ballsbridge Terrace; tel: 01 668 0025; www.thelobsterpot.ie; €€€; Mon–Fri 12.30–2pm, 6–10.30pm, Sat 6.30–10.30pm; bus: 5, 7, 45
Fish-lovers may live to regret not making the trip out to Ballsbridge to uncover one of Dublin's best-kept secrets. An open fire, brass fittings, warm shades and hospitable hosts replicate an

old-fashioned homely atmosphere. Make your selection from the daily catch and have it perfectly cooked to your liking.

Roly's Bistro
7 Ballsbridge Terrace; tel: 01 668 2611; www.rolysbistro.ie; €€–€€€; daily noon–2.45pm, 6–10pm; bus: 5, 7, 45
For many years Roly's has

stood its ground as one of Dublin's most significant restaurants, renowned for its reliable, robust Irish dishes; its selection of freshly baked breads alone is worth the trip out to Ballsbridge. The bright, airy dining room is always busy with locals, and it can get noisy.

A pint of Guinness *(left)*, the craic and an inexpensive wholesome meal; what more could you want? Pub grub is very popular in Dublin, and while it may not offer adventurous dishes, it does give you the chance to sample real local food, such as Irish stew and colcannon (cabbage and potato), and many pubs lay on a value-for-money carvery at lunchtime. Avoid pubs full of tourists or those that have live music, as you may find inflated prices *(see Food and Drink, p.58, and Traditional Pubs, p.118)*.

Shopping

Dublin's two main shopping areas have very different tones that exemplify the city's north–south divide. North of the River Liffey, on O'Connell and Henry streets, large malls suffice for the needs of everyday shoppers looking for high-street brands. South of the river, meanwhile, in and around Grafton Street, several grand designers flaunt their name among individual stores and boutiques. Otherwise, go to Great George's Street South for second-hand and retro clothing and Francis Street for antiques. For specialised shops, see *Food and Drink, p.60, Irish Design, p.74, Literature, p.77*, and *Music, p.92*.

ART AND ANTIQUES
IB Jorgensen Fine Art
16 Herbert Street;
tel: 01 661 9758;
www.jorgensenfineart.com;
Mon–Fri 9am–5.30pm; bus: 10, 10a; map p.137 E1
As this gallery is owned by one of Ireland's most famous fashion designers, you can expect to pay top dollar here, but the fine art displayed includes work from talent such as Jack B. Yeats, Walter Frederick Osborne and Mary Swanzy.

Kerlin Gallery
Anne's Lane, off Anne Street South; tel: 01 670 9093; www.kerlin.ie; Mon–Fri 10am–5.45pm, Sat 11am–4.30pm; bus: 10a, 128, 746; map p.136 C3
This renowned art gallery has been established in Dublin since 1988. The work of some of Ireland's top contemporary artists, such as Paul Seawright, David Godbold and Dorothy Cross, is showcased alongside emerging new artists.

Above: Grafton Street is Dublin's posh shops hub.

O'Sullivan Antiques
43–44 Francis Street; tel: 01 454 1143; www.osullivan antiques.com; Mon–Sat 10am–6pm; bus: 51b, 78a, 121; map p.135 E3
Owner Chantal O'Sullivan is an expert on Irish antiques and is willing to share her knowledge. The shop contains a real mix of exquisite objects, from mahogany furniture to gilt mirrors and delicate glass.

DEPARTMENT STORES
Arnotts
12 Henry Street; tel: 01 805 0400; www.arnotts.ie;

Visit the north side of Merrion Square on a weekend and you will find amateur artists displaying their originals against the park railings, hoping to make a sale. Many of the artists like to chat about their work, and some are more inspiring than others, but it's possible to pick up a bargain. You never know, you could be buying from the next big thing. *See also Parks and Gardens, p.97.*

Mon–Sat 10am–6.30pm, Thur until 8pm, Sun noon–6pm; bus: 10a, 14a, 46a, Luas: Jervis; map. p.132 B2
Since its conception in 1845, this Irish department store has endured a torrid past, including a massive fire in 1894 that nearly destroyed it and the Easter Rising raging on all sides in 1916. But still the dear old favourite survives to supply Dubliners with all their needs. Even if you don't intend to buy, take a peek inside at the octagonal dome that fills the space with light.

Left: the Grafton Street institution Brown Thomas.

map p.132 C1

An Irish institution founded in 1853, Clery's was Dublin's first department store. It has become famous over the decades for its ornate clock suspended outside, a place for couples to rendezvous before a date. After major restoration inside, the striking landmark building conceals a modern shopping experience that caters to all tastes and budgets.

FASHION, SHOES AND ACCESSORIES

Alias Tom

Duke House, Duke Street; tel: 01 671 5443; Mon–Sat 9.30am–6pm, Thur until 8pm; bus: 10a, 128, 746; map p.136 C3

If your taste is a little off-the-wall then this cutting edge men's fashion store is for you. Top international designers such as Armani are on display, but expect big prices to match.

Avoca

11–13 Suffolk Street; tel: 01 677 4215; www.avoca.ie; Mon–Sat 10am–6pm, Thur until 8pm, Sun 11am–6pm; bus: 10a, 13a, 15a; map p.136 C4

From small acorns grow big trees! That is certainly the case with this three-storey department store that is jam-packed to the eaves with Avoca's own, extensive range of truly Irish products.

SEE ALSO IRISH DESIGN, P.74

Brown Thomas

88–95 Grafton Street; tel: 01 605 6666; www.brown thomas.com; Mon 9.30am–7pm, Tue 10am–7pm, Wed–Fri 9.30am–8pm, Thur until 9pm, Sat 9am–7pm, Sun 11am–7pm; bus: 10a, 14a, 70b; map p.136 C3

A sophisticated air and chic surroundings ensure this well-heeled department store is not out of place among the other upmarket stores on Grafton Street. Be

prepared though: the designer clothes, cosmetics and household items for sale here may stretch your overdraft.

Clery's

18–27 Lower O'Connell Street; tel: 01 878 6000; www.clerys.com; Mon–Sat 10am–6.30pm, Thur until 9pm, Sun noon–6pm; bus: 10a, 14a, 46a, Luas: Abbey Street;

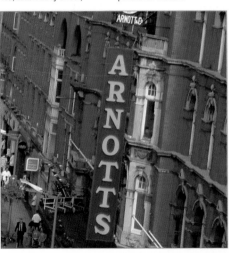

Right: the long-standing department store Arnotts.

A-Wear

26 Grafton Street; tel: 01 472
4960; www.Awear.com;
Mon–Sat 9.30am–7pm, Thur
until 9pm, Sun 11am–6pm;
bus: 10a, 14a, 70b; map. p.136
C3

Whether you've seen your
favourite celebrity wearing
it or it's hot off the cat-
walk, you're sure to find it
here at this popular trend-
setting fashion store. The
low price tags will
impress, too.

Fitzpatrick Shoes

chq Building, Custom House
Quay; tel: 01 859 0370;
www.fitzpatricksshoes.com;
Mon–Sat 10am–6pm, Sun
noon–6pm; bus: 53a, 151,
Luas: George's Dock;
map p.133 E2

Having traded successfully
in Grafton Street for over
70 years, this family-run
business synonymous with
high-quality footwear has
opened another branch in
the chq building. Floating
glass and a white high-
gloss finish provide a perfect showcase for the
fabulous items.

Konfusion

5a Crown Alley; tel: 01 707
1760; www.konfusion.ie;
Mon–Sat 10.30am–6pm, Sun
noon–6pm; bus: 50, 66a, 66b;
map p.136 B1

Bring some sunshine into
your life at this eclectic
shop, selling a range of
unusual and funky clothes
and accessories in vibrant
colours and textures that
will brighten your wardrobe
and your day.

Louis Copeland

39–41 Capel Street; tel: 01 872
1600; www.louiscopeland.com;
Mon–Sat 9am–5.30pm, Thur
until 8pm; bus: 37, 39a, 70a;
map p.132 A1

All well-dressed Irish men
endeavour to own a made-
to-measure suit that carries
the name of this acclaimed
tailor. If you haven't got
time to get measured up,
there is a range by top
designers sold off the peg.

Susan Hunter

13 Westbury Mall, off Grafton
Street; tel: 01 679 1271;
www.susanhunterlingerie.ie;
Mon–Sat 10am–6pm, Thur until
7pm; bus: 10a, 14a, 70b; map
p.136 C3

Splash out and spoil yourself at this small shop
where the fabulous array
of lingerie is irresistible and
the personal service is
second to none. Brands
include La Perla, consid-
ered to be one of the best
in the world.

JEWELLERY
Barry Doyle Design Jewellers

Upstairs, 30 George Street
Arcade, South Great George's
Street; tel: 01 671 2838;
www.barrydoyledesign.com;
Mon–Sat 10am–6pm, Thur until
7pm; bus: 16a, 19a, 83; map
p.136 B3

Check out the stunning
range of silver and gold
jewellery at this studio and
shop in central Dublin.
Barry Doyle and his
partner Adrianna design
and make fabulous items
on request, or you can
choose from the ready-
made collection, which
includes Celtic and
contemporary designs.

Right: flowers and fashion on
Grafton Street.

Left: the impressive Stephen's Green Shopping Centre.

level is turned over to a food court.

SHOPPING CENTRES
Ilac Centre
Henry Street; tel: 01 704 1460; Mon–Sat 9am–6pm, Thur until 9pm, Sun noon–6pm; bus: 10a, 14a, 46a, Luas: Jervis; map p.132 B2

This is the oldest shopping centre in the city centre, but following a recent makeover the brighter modern space has a lot to offer the shopper, including two department stores, Debenhams and Dunnes.

Jervis Centre
Jervis Street; tel: 01 878 1323; www.jervis.ie; Mon–Sat 9am–6.30pm, Thur until 9pm, Fri– Sat until 7pm, Sun 11am–6.30pm; bus: 25a, 66a, 83, Luas: Jervis; map p.132 B1

A big variety of retail outlets, including familiar British names like Marks & Spencer and Next, are housed in this modern complex laid out over three floors – the upper

Powerscourt Townhouse Centre
59 William Street South; tel: 01 671 7000; www.powerscourt centre.com; Mon–Fri 10am– 6pm, Thur until 8pm, Sat 9am–6pm, Sun noon–6pm; bus: 16a, 19a, 83; map p.136 B3

Shopping is a joy at this one-of-a-kind arcade housed in a beautifully renovated 18th-century townhouse, which still retains all its former character. Charming, narrow warrens containing small speciality shops surround an inner courtyard with a café and the upper levels offer further eating and drinking options.

Stephen's Green Shopping Centre
Grafton Street; tel: 01 478 0888; www.stephensgreen.com; Mon–Sat 9am–7pm, Thur until 9pm, Sun 11am–6pm; bus 10a, 14a, 70b; map p.136 C3

Above: in the Powerscourt Townhouse Centre.

You can't overlook this gleaming white, mock-Victorian masterpiece standing at the top end of Grafton Street. Once you're inside, the glass roof, white wrought iron and a huge decorative clock distract from the diverse range of shops. The top-floor restaurant has great views over the Green.

Sports

The Irish are very passionate about sport. Rugby Union, golf and horse racing are what many people associate Ireland with, but there are several other less obvious sporting activities that are well supported both in terms of spectators and participation. The national games of Gaelic football and hurling are Ireland's most widely played sports. Dubliners love their soccer, although most support British teams such as Manchester United and Glasgow Celtic. Sports facilities in the centre are limited, but the suburbs are home to two international stadiums, championship golf courses and renowned racecourses.

GAELIC SPORTS

Promoted by the **Gaelic Athletic Association (GAA)**, the Irish are raised on the fast and furious Gaelic games of **hurling** and **football**. In Dublin the action is focused around the GAA All Ireland Finals, played at **Croke Park** in September. Fanatical sports fans travel from all over the country to be at the finals hoping to see their team victorious. The atmosphere is electric, but tickets are in short supply.

There are many amateur teams in Dublin that play not only hurling and

football but also **carnogie** and **handball**. On a weekend, in open spaces such as Phoenix Park you are likely to see one of these teams practising. Those who want to know more about these unique sports should visit the **GAA Museum** at Croke Park.
SEE ALSO CELTIC ROOTS AND CULTURE, P.38; MUSEUMS AND GALLERIES, P.88

Croke Park Stadium
Croke Park; tel: 01 819 2300; www.crokepark.ie; call or check website for fixtures, stadium tours and tickets; admission charge; bus: 3, 11, 16

Home of the Gaelic Athletic Association.

GOLF
Portmarnock
Portmarnock; tel: 01 846 0611; www.portmarnock.com; daily 7.30am–dusk; green fees charge
Golf packages are available at this luxury resort that features one of Ireland's best links courses, designed by German golfer Bernhard Langer. Located about 15 minutes' drive outside Dublin between Malahide and Howth.

Royal Dublin
Bull Island, Dollymount; tel: 01 833 6346; www.theroyaldublin golfclub.com; daily 8am–dusk; green fees charge
Ireland's oldest golf club has hosted endless major championships and golfing legends since it was founded in 1885. The unique position among the dunes of Bull Island present a challenge to

Left: locals' passion for sports is encouraged early in life.

Left: at a Heineken Cup match at Croke Park.

The supporters of Ireland's most successful soccer team, **Shamrock Rovers**, are still in a state of shock. After years of financial decline the tiny Dublin club has clawed its way back to the top, opening a new stadium in the suburb of Tallaght in 2009. But then, beyond their wildest dreams, it was announced that the team would be playing a pre-season warm up game against Spain's mighty Real Madrid, and the 2009 'World Player of the Year' Cristiano Ronaldo would tread the hallowed turf, making his debut for Real Madrid following his £80 million world-record transfer from Manchester United. The game ended with a 0–1 victory for Real Madrid on 20 July 2009, but it remained an exhilarating day Shamrock Rovers' supporters will never forget.

Left: at a Six Nations rugby match at Croke Park.

tel: 01 668 3502; Wed–Thur, Sat 6.30pm; admission charge; bus: 2, 3, 77
Just a short bus ride to Ringsend, the upgraded facilities at Shelbourne Park provide a fun and exciting evening's entertainment – if your luck's in you might even go home richer.

HORSE RACING
Leopardstown Racecourse
Leopardstown Road, Foxrock; tel: 01 289 0500; www.leopardstown.com; office Mon–Fri 9am–5.30pm, from 8am on race days; admission charge; bus: 86, 118
There is a fantastic atmosphere here on race days.

RUGBY UNION
Irish fans are devoted to rugby, and the season culminates with the All Ireland Finals, while the Six Nations Championship is the highlight of the international rugby year. Details of fixtures are listed in the newspapers, but tickets for any of these games are pretty hard to come by. The national stadium is officially **Lansdowne Road**, but it is currently being rebuilt and the proposed date of completion is early 2010. In the meantime all international rugby continues to take place at the Croke Park stadium *(see opposite)*.

WATER SPORTS
Surfdock
Grand Canal Dock, South Dock Road, Ringsend; tel: 01 668 3945; www.surfdock.ie; admission charge; bus: 2, 3, 77
This water sports specialist offers courses for all levels in windsurfing, water-skiing and kayaking in Dublin's Grand Canal Basin.

any golfer. Non-members are welcome Mon–Tue and Thur–Fri.

GREYHOUND RACING
Harold's Cross
Harold's Cross; tel: 01 497 1081; www.igb.ie/haroldscross; Mon–Tue, Fri 8pm; admission charge; bus: 16, 49
Greyhound racing in Dublin has gained in popularity, so if you fancy a flutter join the lively crowd of Dubliners at this stadium in the southwestern suburbs.

Shelbourne Park
South Lotts Road, Ringsend;

113

Statues and Monuments

Dubliners' affection for their city's statues and monuments has resulted in some quirky nicknames being attributed to them over the years. The city is home to a host of sculpted Irish luminaries, both political and literary, and there are some humorous characters, too. Sculptures act as resting places, such as the whacky bronze palm-tree seat in Temple Bar or the *Joker's Chair* in Merrion Square. On a more serious note, there are monuments in memory of harsher times, of famine, war and political struggle.

IN THE GARDENS

Children of Lír – Garden of Remembrance

Parnell Square East; tel: 01 821 3021; Apr–Sept: daily 8.30am–6pm, Oct–Nov: 9.30am–4pm; free; bus: 1, 2, 14; map p.132 B3

This moving memorial is dedicated to those who died in the pursuit of Irish independence. It recreates the legend of the four children of Lír, who were turned into swans by their jealous stepmother.

Fusiliers' Arch – St Stephen's Green

St Stephen's Green; tel: 01 475 7816; www.heritageireland.ie; Mon–Sat 7.30am–dusk, Sun,

public hols 9.30am–dusk; free; bus: 92, 118, 746; map p.136 C2

This imposing monument to the Royal Dublin Fusiliers killed during the Boer War is still referred to as Traitor's Gate, a reference to the conscription or enlistment of Irishmen enforced by the British army in wartime.

Oscar Wilde – Merrion Square

Merrion Square; tel: 01 222 5278; daily 10am–dusk; free; bus: 45; map p.137 D3

Surely the most sublime statue in the city, Oscar Wilde lies languishing on a rock, dressed in a velvet smoking jacket with an

inscrutable smile on his face. It is particularly life-like, and even more evocative by night.

SEE ALSO PARKS AND GARDENS, P.97

O'CONNELL STREET

Charles Stewart Parnell

O'Connell Street; bus: 14a, 16a, 746; map p.132 B3

Augustus Saint-Gaudens' striking monument to the

While a statue of poet Patrick Kavanagh *(see right)* relaxes by the Grand Canal, a very life-like Brendan Behan is settled on a bench by the Royal Canal, just off Dorset Street to the north of the city centre. The well-known poet, novelist and drinker can be found in 'conversation' with a bird perched on the bench beside him. The location is not far from Mountjoy Prison, where Behan was an inmate in the 1940s for Republican activities. The charming statue belies a chequered life cut short by alcohol abuse at the age of 41.

Left: The Fusiliers' Arch honours fallen Boer War soldiers.

Left: the 'Tart with the Cart' on Grafton Street.

Meeting Place

Liffey Street Lower; bus: 25a, 66a, 67a; map p.132 B1
Jakki Mckenna's evocative ladies, fondly known as the 'Hags with the Bags' (1988), bring a touch of humour to shopping north of the river.

FACT AND FICTION
Molly Malone

Grafton Street; bus: 10a, 13a, 15a; map p.136 C4
Another statue erected in 1988 brought the eponymous fishmonger with the ample cleavage to the streets of Dublin. More often referred to as the 'Tart with the Cart', Molly is believed to have lived and worked in Dublin until her death in 1734.

Patrick Kavanagh

Wilton Terrace; bus: 10, 10a; map p.137 E1
Enjoying the place he loved, poet Patrick Kavanagh or the 'Crank on the Bank' relaxes on a bench by the Grand Canal.

Left: the striking Spire on O'Connell Street.

p.132 C2
Known irreverently by Dubliners as the 'Prick with the Stick', Marjorie Fitzgibbon's bronze statue (1979) shows literary genius Joyce in nonchalant pose with a walking cane.

The Spire

O'Connell Street; bus: 10a, 14a, 46a; map p.132 C2
This striking steel monument, also known as the **Monument of Light** (2003) or by the nickname 'The Spike', is 3m (10ft) at the base, rising 120m (394ft) to a pinnacle of only 15cm (6in). It sways gently, but safely, in the breeze.

ALONG THE QUAYS
Famine Figures

Custom House Quay; bus: 53a, 151; map p.131 D1
Sculpted by Rowan Gillespie, the desolate figures depicted in *Famine* (1997) represent the suffering of Great Famine of 1845–9.

'uncrowned king of Ireland' and fighter for home rule marks the end of O'Connell Street.

Daniel O'Connell

O'Connell Street; bus: 10a, 14a, 46a; map p.132 C1
The bronze statue of this hero of the people, and one of Ireland's most famous patriots and politicians, stands atop a memorial depicting four angels representing the four provinces of Ireland.

James Joyce

Earl Street, just off O'Connell Street; bus: 10a, 14a, 46a; map

Below: the Famine Figures on Custom House Quay.

Theatre and Dance

Early playwrights from Dublin, such as Richard Brinsley Sheridan, set the stage for a cultural phenomenon that culminated in the 20th century with some of the most famous names in modern literature, such as Wilde, Shaw, O'Casey and Beckett. The genre befits the Irish sense of wit and drama, and today a variety of venues in the city stage conventional and fringe theatre. Dance ranges from ballet and modern to the traditional Irish dancing made popular by *Riverdance*. See also *Festivals and Events, p.54* and *Literature, p.76*.

DUBLIN THEATRE

It's not only the playwrights that have raised the profile of drama performed on stage in Dublin. Some great actors have performed in the city, and it is a popular venue for high-profile and classical performers. **Peter O'Toole** performed in **Sean O'Casey's** *Juno and the Paycock* at the Gaiety in 1969, and in **Samuel Beckett's** *Waiting for Godot* at the Abbey in 1970. Members of the famous **Cusack** acting dynasty from Dalkey started out by treading the boards in Dublin's theatres, and **Sir Michael Gambon**

began his career in the Gaiety Theatre in 1962.

Whatever your taste in theatre, be it drama, musicals or readings, there are historic theatres, modern arts centres and small intimate venues, such as Bewleys Café Theatre, to chose from.

DUBLIN DANCE

Some of the larger productions, such as those performed by visiting ballet companies and the hugely popular *Riverdance*, are staged at the larger arenas in Dublin, Helix and The O2 *(see Music, p.92)*. The main centre for modern dance is

the Dance Theatre of Ireland, located outside Dublin at Dún Laoghaire. It is home to the DYDC (Dublin Youth Dance Company). Traditional Irish dancing is performed at hotels, pubs and various venues in the city, and classes are run at the Comhaltas Regional Resource Centre *(see Celtic Roots and Culture, p.39).*

VENUES

Abbey Theatre and Peacock Theatre
26 Lower Abbey Street; tel: 01 887 2200; www.abbeytheatre.ie; box office: Mon–Sat 10am–7pm (collect tickets during the hour

> Central to Trinity College's Department of Drama (www.tcd.ie/drama) is the **Samuel Beckett Theatre**, opened in 1992. During term-time it showcases the work of students, and in university vacations it plays host to visiting theatre companies from around the world. It is also involved in the mainstream and fringe theatre festivals.

Left: the Gaiety Theatre stages a variety of performances.

4045; www.gate-theatre.ie; box office: Mon–Sat 10am–7pm (collect tickets up until performance start time); bus: 16a, 41, 746; map p.132 B3
The Gate was established in 1928 and continues to promote both a modern and traditional Irish repertoire. In 1991 the Gate presented a full retrospective of the 19 stage plays of Samuel Beckett. It also has a long association with Irish playwright Brian Friel.

Olympia
72 Dame Street; tel: 01 679 3323; www.olympia.ie; box office: daily 10.30am–6.30pm (no shows), 10.30–9pm (show days; collect during hour before show); bus: 50, 56a, 123; map p.136 A1
One of the oldest theatres in Dublin, the Olympia hosts a programme of traditional plays, musicals and dance troupes.

Project Arts Centre
39 Essex Street East; tel: 01 881 9613; www.projectarts centre.ie; times vary according to art exhibitions and evening performance, see website or call in advance; bus: 50, 66a, 78a; map p.136 A1
Cutting-edge drama along with music and dance is performed here.

Left: a performance at the Ulster Bank Dublin Theatre Festival *(see p.55)*.

before curtain up); bus: 42, 43, 130, Luas: Abbey Street; map p.133 C1
Within the same premises, the Abbey and the Peacock theatres cover a wide spectrum of drama. The Abbey opened its doors on this site in 1966, but the original theatre, founded by W. B. Yeats and Lady Augusta Gregory in 1903, was in Old Abbey Street. The Abbey, together with the Peacock, which stages new plays, form the National Theatre of Ireland. Plans to move to a new site in Docklands are still ongoing.

Gaiety Theatre
King Street South; tel: 01 679 5622; www.gaietytheatre.com; box office: Mon–Sat 10am–6pm (or performance start time); bus: 92, 118, 746; map p.136 B3
A wonderfully diverse pro-

Tickets for major productions can be bought online from internet providers such as **Ticketmaster** (www.ticket master.ie) or at their outlets in the city, including the Dublin Tourism Centre in Suffolk Street. Ticketron outlets can be found in the Jervis Shopping Centre and Stephen's Green Shopping Centre *(see Shopping, p.111).*

gramme has graced this fine building since its inauguration in 1871. Plays, musicals and dance feature here.

Gate Theatre
1 Cavendish Row; tel: 01 874

Right: the Olympia.

Traditional Pubs

The pub is synonymous with Ireland as Guinness and surely ranks in the top five of most people's lists of what to visit while in Dublin. Although a good deal of the traditional pubs in the city have been brought into the 21st century and lost their spit-and-sawdust origins, there are many that have retained their original fittings and typical Irish atmosphere. Traditional music continues to play an important role in pub culture, and at many establishments you will find customers clapping along to the beat while drinking a pint of Guinness and sharing the craic with a friend.

FAR WEST AND PHOENIX PARK

Ryan's of Parkgate Street

28 Parkgate Street; tel: 01 677 6097; Mon–Wed 3–11.30pm, Thur noon–11.30pm, Fri–Sat noon–12.30am, Sun 12.30–11pm; bus: 66, Luas: Heuston; map p.130 B1

This is one of the finest Victorian pubs in Dublin, dating from 1896. Its interior boasts antique brass lamps and mirrors, plus a wonderful carved oak and

Below: Davy Byrnes is mentioned in *Ulysses*.

mahogany horseshoe-shaped bar. The elegant FXB Steak and Seafood Restaurant is located upstairs.

SOUTH OF THE LIFFEY, WEST

Brazen Head

Bridge Street; tel: 01 677 9549; www.brazenhead.com; Mon–Sat 10.30am–midnight, Sun noon–midnight; bus: 25, 69x; map p.135 E4

Reputedly Dublin's oldest pub, established in 1198, the Brazen Head oozes old-world charm. It hosts some of the best traditional music in the city, with sessions every night and featured bands at the weekends. There's good wholesome food in the restaurant, too – Irish stew and Guinness is a winning combination – or pub snacks in the bar.

CENTRAL CORE, SOUTH OF THE LIFFEY

The Auld Dubliner

24–25 Temple Bar; tel: 01 677 0527; Mon–Thur 10.30am–11.30pm, Fri–Sat

10.30am–12.30am, Sun 12.30pm–11pm; bus: 50, 66a, 66b; map p.136 B1

The unusual pub sign, complete with clock, will guide you to a warm welcome at the Auld Dubliner in the heart of Temple Bar. Enjoy a drink in the attractive traditional bar or a meal of hearty Irish food, plus daily Irish music sessions.

Davy Byrnes

21 Duke Street; tel: 01 677 5217; www.davybyrnes.com; Mon–Wed 11am–11.30pm, Thur–Fri 11am–12.30am, Sat 10.30am–12.30am, Sun 12.30pm–11pm; bus: 10a, 128, 746; map p.136 C3

The lovely bar, with its glorious stained-glass ceiling, is popular with followers of James Joyce. This was a favourite haunt of Joyce, and it makes an appearance in his famous novel *Ulysses*. It is, however, a special spot for Dubliners, too, with its location close to the shopping and office areas.

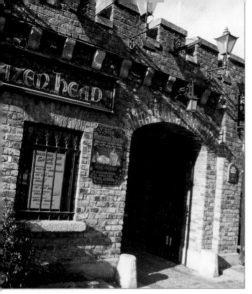

Left: Dublin's oldest pub, the Brazen Head.

McDaids

3 Harry Street; tel: 01 679 4395; Mon–Thur 10.30am–11.30pm, Fri–Sat 10.30am–12.30am, Sun 12.30pm–11pm; bus: 10a, 14a, 70b; map p.136 C3

This is another of Dublin's great literary pubs, particularly known for its association with the writer Brendan Behan. It's a no-frills pub with a quiet bar upstairs and a buzzing atmosphere downstairs.

Mulligan's

8 Poolbeg Street; tel: 01 677 5582; www.mulligans.ie; Mon–Wed 10.30am–11.30pm, Thur–Sat 10.30am–12.30am, Sun 12.30pm–11pm; bus: 1, 2, 50, DART: Tara Street; map p.133 D1

Mulligan's is one of the most characterful pubs in Dublin and has been frequented by some famous names in past, including John F. Kennedy and James Joyce. It's popular with journalists, who happily rub shoulders with students and visitors.

Above: McDaids, a Brendan Behan favourite.

Farrington's

28 Essex Street East; tel: 01 671 5135; Mon–Thur 10.30am–11.30pm, Fri–Sat 10.30am–2.30am, Sun 12.30pm–11pm; bus: 50, 66a, 78a; map p.136 A1

Named after a character in James Joyce's *Dubliners*, Farrington's retains its original Victorian splendour. Its downstairs bar is good for a smooth pint, some gentle craic and regular live-music sessions.

Kehoe's

9 Anne Street South; tel: 01 677 8312; Mon–Thur 10.30am–11.30pm, Fri–Sat 10.30am–12.30am, Sun 12.30pm–11pm; bus: 10a, 128, 746; map p.136 C3

With its narrow bar and an intimate snug, Kehoe's is the epitome of the traditional pub, unspoilt and a great place to sample a beautifully poured pint of Guinness. It's often packed solid, so go on a weekday if you want some space to appreciate the cracking ambience.

The Long Hall

51 South Great George's Street; tel: 01 475 1590; Mon–Wed 4–11.30pm, Thur 1pm–11.30pm, Fri–Sat 1pm–12.30am, Sun 1pm–11pm; bus: 16a, 19a, 83; map p.136 B3

This pub is one of the few remaining untouched Victorian pubs in the city. As the name suggests, the mirrored bar is very long, and the decoration is magnificent, exhibiting fine plasterwork on the ceiling, chandeliers, paintings, muskets and other paraphernalia.

There is a trend in Dublin for a return to the small breweries, or microbreweries as they are now called, to bring a traditional brew back to the city. The Porterhouse Brewing Company has several bars serving their nine different beers, while **Messrs Maguire** (1–2 Burgh Quay; tel: 01 670 5777; www.messrsmaguire.ie; Mon–Tue 10.30am–12.30am, Wed 10.30am–1.30am, Thur–Sat 10.30am–2.30am, Sun noon–midnight; bus: 14, 46a, 48a, DART: Tara Street; map p.133 C1) on Burgh Quay serves eight of their own beers made on the premises.

Left: Oliver St John Gogarty in Temple Bar.

Although very much geared to entertaining tourists, this is still a traditional pub but with noise and crowds, plus traditional music sessions every night of the week. SEE ALSO HOTELS, P.69

The Stag's Head

1 Dame Court, tel: 01 679 3687; www.thestagshead.ie; daily 10.30am–late; bus: 50, 56a, 123; map p.136 B4
Considered one of the finest in the city, The Stag's Head is everything you would expect from a traditional Dublin pub. Its fabulous stained glass, mounted stag's head, beautiful mahogany bar and intimate snugs create a first-class backdrop for the regular traditional music sessions.

The Temple Bar

47–48 Temple Bar; tel: 01 672 5286; www.thetemplepubdublin.com; Mon–Thur 10.30am–2.30am, Fri–Sat 10.30am–1.30am, Sun noon–12.30am; bus: 50, 66a, 66b; map p.136 A1
Proud owners of the 'Traditional Irish Music Pub of the Year' award from 2002 to 2009, this is a great place to come and listen to the sounds of the *bodhrán*, fiddle, tin whistle and more. You can wash down oysters with your Guinness as you listen or take a break in the courtyard beer garden.

ST STEPHEN'S GREEN AND AROUND

O'Donoghue's

15 Merrion Row; tel: 01 660 7194; www.odonoghues.ie;

Neary's

1 Chatham Street; tel: 01 677 8596; Sun–Thur 10.30am–11.30pm, Fri–Sat 10.30am–12.30am; bus: 92, 118, 746; map p.136 C3
In the same ownership for over 50 years, Neary's bohemian ambience draws poets and literary types to its unspoilt Edwardian interior. Being close to the Gaiety Theatre it is also a favourite with actors and theatregoers.

Old Stand

37 Exchequer Street; tel: 01 677 7220; www.theoldstandpub.com; Mon–Thur 10.30am–11.30pm, Fri–Sat 10.30am–12.30am, Sun noon–11pm; bus: 16a, 19a, 83; map p.136 B4
There has been a pub on this site for over 300 years, and the Old Stand retains a cosy local feeling. It has particular links to Dublin's rugby fraternity, hence its name, and it is a popular venue before and after internationals at Lansdowne Road.

Oliver St John Gogarty

58–59 Fleet Street; tel: 01 671 1822; www.gogartys.ie/pub; Mon–Sat 10.30am–2.30am, Sun noon–1.30am; bus: 46, 150, 746; map p.136 B1
Gogarty is named after the Irish poet, playwright and surgeon, and is located in the heart of Temple Bar.

Below: pulling a pint at O'Donoghue's.

Right: The Temple Bar.

120

Mon–Thur 10.30am–11.30am, Fri–Sat 10.30am–12.30am, Sun noon–11pm; bus: 10a; map p.137 D2

The legendary band The Dubliners helped put this pub on the map, and tourists from all over the world flock here for some of the best traditional Irish music sessions in the city. It's also popular with rugby-lovers, who gather here on international days. The tiny bar gets packed to the rafters in the evenings.

Toner's Museum Pub

139 Baggot Street Lower; tel: 01 676 3090; Mon–Wed 10.30am–11.30am, Thur–Sat 10.30am–12.30am, Sun 12.30pm–11pm; bus: 10, 10a; map p.137 E2

This pub manages to retain a real sense of old-world charm. It is named after James Toner, the licensee in the 1920s, who ran it as a bar and grocery shop. This is another pub once frequented by literary greats, including W.B. Yeats and Patrick Kavanagh.

DOCKLANDS AND CANALS

Doheny & Nesbitt

5 Baggot Street Lower; tel: 01 676 2945; Mon–Thur 10.30am–12.30am, Fri–Sat 10.30am–12.30am, Sun noon–11pm; bus: 10, 10a; map p.137 E1

Politicians, lawyers and journalists setting the world to rights have long frequented this distinguished drinking emporium, set off the tourist trail. Spread over three floors, its Victorian origins are reflected in the high ceilings, intimate snugs and mirrored walls.

O'Brien's Ferryman

35 Sir John Rogerson Quay; tel: 01 671 7053; Mon–Thur 10.30am–11.30am, Fri–Sat 10.30am–12.30am, Sun 12.30–11pm; bus: 3

O'Brien's is now a far cry from its role in the former no-go dockland area of Dublin. The area has been 'gentrified', but the pub has managed to retain the traditional feel of a local and offers a friendly welcome.

There are several walking tours involving pubs in Dublin; the tourist information office in Suffolk Street has information. You can choose from a **Traditional Irish Musical Pub Crawl** or the more academic **Dublin Literary Pub Crawl**. Pints of Guinness are not compulsory at every port of call, unless so desired *(see also Walks, Bus Tours and Boat Trips, p.124, 126)*.

NORTH OF THE LIFFEY, WEST

Kavanagh's (Gravediggers)

1 Prospect Square, Glasnevin; tel: 01 830 7978; Mon–Thur 10.30am–11.30am, Fri–Sat 10.30am–midnight, Sun 12.30pm–11pm; bus: 13, 19, 40, train: Drumcondra

Now in the sixth generation of the same family, Kavanagh's (located next door to Glasnevin Cemetery) is an utterly unspoilt Victorian gem. Add to this no music, piped or otherwise, and one of the best pints in the city, and it is worth the effort to visit the suburb of Glasnevin.

Transport

Dublin is accessible by both air and sea, with the airport and two ferry terminals close to the centre. Due to its compact centre, Dublin is easy to navigate on foot, which is undoubtedly the best way to absorb this city's special personality. The main roads in the city have cycle lanes, making it safe and convenient for those who choose to travel on two wheels. Inevitably, if you want to see all the sights you'll need to utilise public transport. An efficient network of buses combined with Luas trams and the DART railway ensure that nowhere in and around Dublin ever seems too far away. See also *Walks, Bus Tours and Boat Trips, p.124*.

GETTING THERE

BY AIR

Dublin Airport (tel: 01 814 111; www.dublinairport.com) is 11km (7 miles) north of the city. There are direct flights between Britain, mainland Europe and North America, and connecting flights from New Zealand, Australia and Asia.

Airlink bus services Nos. 747 and 748 run frequently from the airport to the central bus station and **Heuston Railway Station**, and take about 20–30 minutes, costing €6 one way.

An alternative is the **Aircoach** (tel: 01 844 7118; www.aircoach.ie), which leaves at 15–20-minute intervals, 24 hours a day, costing €7 one way. The coach makes several designated stops throughout the city and continues on to Ballsbridge.

Taxis to the city centre leave from outside the Arrivals area. The cost to the city centre is generally about €30–35, but double-check the price before you

Above: a Luas tram.

get in. All of the main car-hire companies have offices in the Arrivals Hall.

BY SEA

All year round, six different ferry companies sail from the UK into the ports of Dublin and Dún Laoghaire (12km/7½ miles from the centre), with up to 18 daily sailings between them. The journey takes around 3 hours 15 minutes on a traditional ferry, or 1 hour 45 minutes via the high-speed options.

Taxis and buses operate from both ports into the city centre, or from Dún Laoghaire terminal the DART railway can easily be accessed.

Irish Ferries
tel: 01 819 3942;
www.www.irishferries.com

Isle of Man Steam Packet Company
tel: 01624 661661;
www.steam-package.com

Norfolk Irish Sea
tel: 01 819 2999;
www.norfolkline.com

P&O Irish Sea
tel: 01 407 3434;
www.poirishsea.com

Stena Line
tel: 01 204 7777;
www.stenaline.co.uk

BY TRAIN

There are two mainline stations in Dublin: trains from the north arrive at **Connolly Station**, which is right in the centre of the city, and trains from the

Left: ferries sail across the Irish Sea several times a day.

BY DART

The DART railway follows the coast from Malahide in the north to Greystones in the south, stopping at 25 coastal suburbs in between; it is more useful to commuters who use it on a daily basis rather than the tourist, unless you are heading to the coast. Trains run every five or 10 minutes during peak times. Tickets are inexpensive and can be purchased from machines at the station.

SEE ALSO DART EXCURSIONS, P.44; ENVIRONMENT, P.48

If you want to hire a quality bike fitted with all the equipment needed for either a day trip out or a cycling holiday, check out **Cycleways** (185–186 Parnell Street; tel: 01 873 4748; www.cycleways.com; Mon–Sat 9.30am–6pm, Thur until 8pm, Sun 11am–5pm). *See also Environment, p.48.*

south and west arrive at **Heuston Station**, which has excellent public transport links just outside.

GETTING AROUND

BY BUS

City buses, run by **Dublin Bus** (55 O'Connell Street; tel: 01 873 4222; www.dublinbus.ie), are inexpensive and operate between Mon–Sat 6am–11.30pm and Sun 10am–11.30pm, with a limited **Nitelink** service to the suburbs until 4.30am Thur–Sat. If you see 'An Lar' on the front of a bus, this means city centre.

Tickets are sold at Dublin Bus, on some newsstands and on board with the exact change.

Bus Éireann (Amiens Street; tel: 01 836 6111; www.buseireann.ie) runs a nationwide service out of the main bus terminus on Amiens Street, a short walk from O'Connell Street.

BY LUAS

Cutting through the city starting at Connolly Station, the Luas (www.luas.ie) transit system is a highly modern light-rail service with strategic stops in the centre continuing out to the suburbs.

BY TAXI

Taxis can be found at various points in the city, and there are stands outside train and bus stations, so it is generally easy to find a cab, although queues can be long at club kicking-out time. Taxis are licensed and metered, but additional charges will be made for luggage, travelling on a Sunday or after 10pm.

City Cabs
tel: 01 872 7272

NRC
tel: 01 677 2222

Right: a packed taxi rank.

Walks, Bus Tours and Boat Trips

O ne of the best ways of getting an insight into the 'real' Dublin is by taking one of the numerous tours on offer. The variety is excellent, particularly when it comes to tours on foot. Whether you want to delve into the turbulent history of the city's past, learn more about Dublin's literary greats or take a pub crawl through the streets, there is something for all tastes. Several bus tours give you the opportunity to see beyond the main attractions and a trip down the River Liffey opens up an alternative way to view the cityscape.

ON FOOT

Dublin Footsteps Walking Tours

Bewley's Café, Grafton Street; tel: 01 496 0641; June–Sept Mon, Wed–Sat 10.30am; admission charge; bus: 10a, 14a, 70b; map p.136 C3

Grab a cup of coffee at Bewleys *(see Bars and Cafés, p.32)* before setting out for a couple of hours walking in the footsteps of the most famous Irish

Below: Dublin offers a range of great walking tours.

writers. The tour takes you around the best of Georgian architecture and the guide gives an informative and entertaining view of the city.

Dublin Literary Pub Crawl

Duke Pub, Duke Street; tel: 01 670 5602; www.dublinpub crawl.com; Apr–Nov daily 7.30pm, Dec–Mar Thur–Sat 7.30pm; admission charge; bus: 10a, 128, 746; map p.136 C3

This tour is great fun: it starts at the Duke and crawls from pub to pub with professional actors performing from the works of Dublin's most famous writers, featuring Oscar Wilde, James Joyce and many more. There's plenty of singing, wit, craic and, if you wish, drinking too.

Historical Walking Tour of Temple Bar

Temple Bar Information Centre, 12 Essex Street East; tel: 01 677 2397; www.visit-temple bar.com; daily regular tours, check for times; admission charge; bus: 50, 66a, 78a; map

All the addresses given in this chapter are the actual point of departure for the tour. Most tours can be booked in advance, through the website, or at the **Dublin Tourism Centre** *(see also Essentials, p.53)*. Many of the tours do not need advance booking, so just turn up on the day.

p.136 A1

Learn more about the most popular tourist destination in Dublin. The tour, lasting one and half hours, takes in all the colourful history of Temple Bar, plus a visit to the major sites close by.

James Joyce Walking Tours

James Joyce Centre, 35 North Great George's Street; tel: 01 878 8457; www.jamesjoyce.ie; Tue, Thur, Sat 11am, 2pm; admission charge; bus: 40a; map p.132 C3

There are a variety of Joyce-themed walking tours, with some following in the footsteps of Leopold Bloom, the hero

Left: guides in character on the Dublin Literary Pub Crawl.

Sandemans New Dublin Tours

City Hall, Dame Street; www.newdublintours.com; daily 11am; free; bus: 50, 56a, 123; map p.136 B4

Just look for the red New Europe T-shirts near the City Hall and join this free tour that works on a tips-only basis, meaning the guides are good. The three-hour tour covers some of the lesser-known sights in the city, while still visiting the most famous attractions.

of Joyce's *Ulysses*. Other walks include the Joyce Circular, which takes you round highlights in Joyce's life. Check the website or at the centre for choices.

Paddy Liddy's Walking Tours

Dublin Tourism Centre, Suffolk Street; www.walkingtours.ie; May–Oct daily, check for individual tour times; admission charge; bus: 10a, 13a, 15a, DART: Tara Street; map p.136 C4

No booking is required for a great range of tours that leave from the tourist office. Pat Liddy, the well-known Dublin historian, author and artist has compiled all the award-winning walks, and at present there are eight diverse subjects to choose from.

1916 Rebellion Walking Tours

23 Wicklow Street; tel: 0868 583847; www.1916rising.com; Mar–Oct Mon–Sat 11.30am, Sun 1pm; admission charge; bus: 10a, 14a, 70b; map p.136 C4;

Starting at the International Bar in Wicklow Street, you will be taken by writers, who are experts on the Easter Rising, to the relevant sites of the historic rebellion. Taken at a leisurely pace, the tour lasts around two hours, and the lively commentary makes for a fascinating insight into Dublin's turbulent past.

The Story of Irish Food Walking tour

Trinity College front gate; tel: 0876 889412; www.histori calinsights.ie; Sat 11.30am, Nov–Mar Fri–Sun 11am; admission charge; bus: 10a, 13a, 15a, DART: Pearse; map p.136 C4

This excellent tour traces the history of Dublin through all aspects of food and drink, revealing how attitudes to consumption have shaped Irish society.

Below: embrace *Ulysses* on a James Joyce Walking Tour.

If you want to get off the beaten track and explore the 'real' Dublin, try one of the walking tours offered by the **Hidden Dublin Walks Ltd** (www.hiddendublinwalks.com). The tours include 'Haunted Dublin' and 'Sexual Dublin', as well as history tours covering Viking, medieval and 19th-century Dublin, and the fight for Irish independence. The history tours are free; the others carry a charge.

During the two-and-a-half-hour tour you will learn about the earliest favourites to the latest celebrity chefs and Dublin restaurants. The tour includes tastings at the wonderful Temple Bar food market.

SEE ALSO FOOD AND DRINK, P.58; RESTAURANTS, P.100

Traditional Irish Musical Pub Crawl
Oliver St John Gogarty Pub,

Fleet Street; tel: 01 475 3313; www.discoverdublin.ie; May–Oct daily 7.30pm, Nov–Apr Thur–Sat 7.30pm; admission charge; bus: 46, 150, 746; map p.136 B1
The crawl kicks off at Gogarty pub *(see Traditional Pubs, p.120)* in Temple Bar. Two professional musicians tell the story of Irish music through word, instrumental tunes and song as you walk from pub to pub. Add a pint or two of Guinness and you are in for a great night out. It's best to arrive early, as these tours are popular, or buy your tickets in advance at the tourist office.

BY BUS
Hop-on, hop-off buses
Two companies run open-top buses in the city. **City Sightseeing** (www.city-sightseeing.com) leaves from outside Dublin Tourism Office *(see Essentials, p.53)* at 14

Upper O'Connell Street and departs daily every 6–8 minutes.

The **Dublin Bus Tour** (www.dublinsightseeing.ie) departs from outside the Bus Information Office at 59 Upper O'Connell Street daily from 9.30am. It's a great way to see the city, with more than 20 stops at Dublin's top attractions. You can hop on and off, and the ticket is valid for 24 hours. The complete tour lasts around 90 minutes, with commentary in several languages.

Ghostbus
Dublin Bus, 59 Upper O'Connell Street; tel: 873 4222; www.dublinsightseeing.ie; Mon–Thur 8pm, Fri 8pm, 8.30pm, Sat–Sun 7pm, 9.30pm; admission charge; bus: 14a, 16a, 746; map p.132 C2

Left: a pub crawl could reveal much of the city's character.

in Bus Tour

Every 10 minutes 24 hour

Run by the city's Dublin Bus *(see opposite)*, the Ghostbus tour takes around two hours. Be prepared to be spooked with tales of fiends and phantoms, body-snatchers and haunted cemeteries. You

Left: the Dublin Bus Tour is a hop-on, hop-off service.

will learn more of Bram Stoker's infamous Dracula character's Dublin origins, and professional actors complete the spooky experience.

Rock'n'Roll, Writers Bus Tour

Westmoreland Street; tel: 01 620 3929; www.dublinrock tour.ie; Wed–Sun noon, 2pm, 4pm, 6pm; admission charge, advance booking advised; bus: 46, 150, 746; map p.132 C1

A highly original bus tour presenting 75 minutes of Dublin's musical and literary heritage with characters as diverse as Thin Lizzy, U2 and James Joyce. Aboard the rock'n'roll bus, which has been shipped over from Tennessee, you will pass along the Dublin streets where legends have walked.

ON THE WATER

Liffey River Cruise

The Boardwalk, Bachelors Walk; tel: 01 473 4082; www.liffeyrivercruises.com; Mar–Nov daily, check for times; admission charge; bus: 39b; map p.132 C1

All aboard the *Spirit of Docklands* for a tour of the river, revealing the history of the Liffey from the Vikings to the recent redevelopment of Dublin's Docklands. The mooring on Bachelors Walk is close to O'Connell Bridge.

Viking Splash

St Stephen's Green North (start point); tel: 01 707 6000; www.vikingsplash.ie; Mar–Nov daily, check website or call for times; admission charge; bus: 92, 118, 746; map p.136 C2

If you are looking for a unique Dublin tour, the Viking Splash certainly offers an unusual way to get around the city. Take the World War II amphibious vehicle by land and water and learn all about Viking Dublin. The splash part of the tour takes you into the Grand Canal at Docklands. Reservations advised.
SEE ALSO CHILDREN, P.41

Below: on board a Liffey River Cruise.

Atlas

The following streetplan of Dublin makes it easy to find the attractions listed in the A–Z section. A selective index to streets and sights will help you find other locations throughout the city.

Map Legend

Motorway		Railway	
Dual carriageway		Dart	
Main road		Post office	
Minor road		Bus station	
Footpath		Airport	
Luas tram	ABBEY	Tourist information	
Pedestrian area		Sight of interest	
Notable building		Cathedral/church	
Park		Museum/gallery	
Hotel		Theatre/concert hall	
Urban area		Synagogue	
Non urban area		Statue/monument	
Cemetery		Hospital	

p130	p131	p132	p133
p134	p135	p136	p137

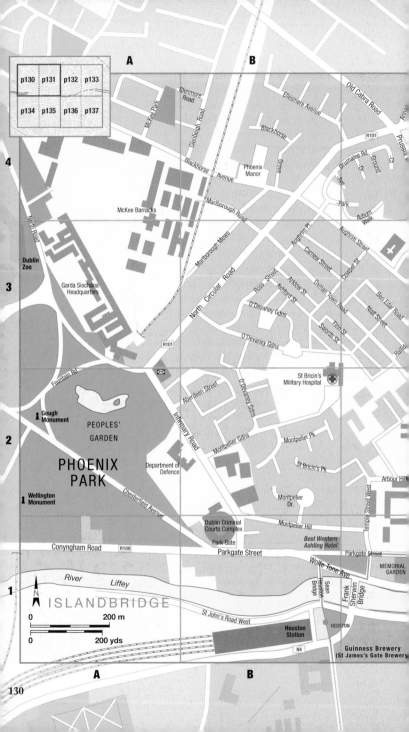

Blessington
Street Basin

Eccles Street

N1

Temple Theatre

Temple Street
Children's Hospital

St Joseph's Parade

Nelson Street

Blessington Street

Dorset Street Upper

Temple Street North

Hardwicke Street

Frederick St North

Belvedere
College

Denmark Street Great

Gardiner Street Upper

Gardiner Pl

Hill Street

Grenville St

4

Wellington Street

Fontenoy Street

Wellington Street

Western Way

Black Church

KING'S

INN

R108

PARK

Dominick Street Upper

Mountjoy Street

Granby Row

Dublin
Writers
Museum

Dublin City
Hugh Lane
Gallery

GARDEN OF
REMEMBRANCE

Parnell Sq
North

Dublin
County
Council

Rutland Place West

N. Cr. George's Street

Hotel
St George

James Joyce
Centre

Parnell Square East

Street

3

King's Inns

Henrietta Street

Law
Library

St Saviour's

Dominick Street Lower

Dominick Place

King's Inns Street

Rotunda
Hospital

Parnell Square West

Gate
Theatre

Cassidys
Hotel

Parnell

Best Western
Academy Plaza

Parnell
Monument

Police
Station

Coleraine Street

Bolton Street

Henrietta Place

College of
Technology

Loftus Lane

Parnell
Centre

Parnell Street

Moore Street

Moore Lane

Cathal Brugha St

O'Connell Street

The Gresham

Savoy
Cinema

St Mary's
Pro-Cathedral

Marlborough Street

2

King Street North

Halston Street

Green Street

Little Britain St

Cuckoo Lane

Jervis Lane Upper

Jervis Lane Lower

Jervis Street

Ilac Centre

Henry Street

The Spire

James
Joyce

Earl St
North

General
Post Office

Mary's Lane

Fish
Market

Fruit and
Vegetable
Market

Arran Street East

Capel Street

Mary's Abbey

St Mary's
Abbey

St Mary's

Jervis
Centre

Mary Street

Liffey Street Upper

Jervis

Princes Street North

Abbey Street Middle

Lotts

Clery's

ABBEY

Daniel
O'Connell

O'Connell
Street

1

N

0   200 m

0   200 yds

Abbey Street Upper

Liffey Street Lower

JERVIS

Swifts Row

Strand Street Great

Morrison
Hotel

Ormond Quay Lower

Grattan Br.

Mary's Abbey

Millennium Bridge

Ha'penny Br. (Liffey Br.)

River   Liffey

Bachelors Walk

Aston Quay

O'Connell
Bridge

Westmoreland St

Fleet Street

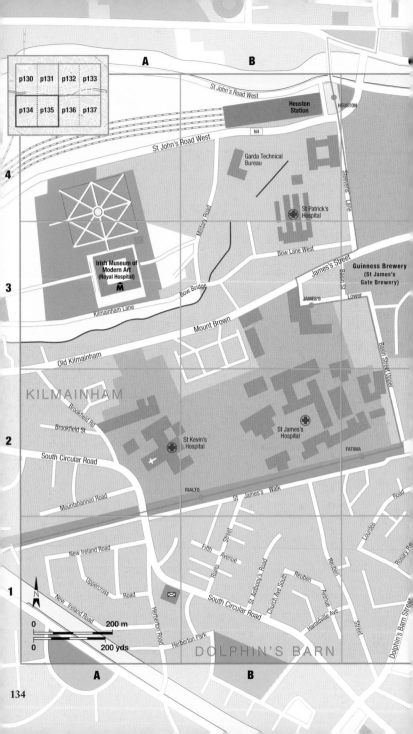

St John's Road West

Heuston Station

HEUSTON

N4

St John's Road West

4

Garda Technical Bureau

St Patrick's Hospital

Steevens Lane

Bow Lane West

Irish Museum of Modern Art (Royal Hospital)

Military Road

James's Street

Basin St

Guinness Brewery (St James's Gate Brewery)

JAMES'S

Lower

3

Bow Bridge

Kilmainham Lane

Mount Brown

Old Kilmainham

Basin Street Upper

KILMAINHAM

Brookfield Rd

Brookfield St

St Kevin's Hospital

St James's Hospital

FATIMA

2

South Circular Road

Mountshannon Road

RIALTO

St James's Walk

New Ireland Road

Fifth Avenue

Rialto Street

St Anthony's Road

Church Ave South

Reuben Street

Reuben Avenue

Lourdes Road

Rosary Rd

Uppercross Road

1

N

New Ireland Road

Herberton Road

Herberton Park

South Circular Road

Hardiville Ave

Dolphin's Barn Street

0 ___ 200 m

0 ___ 200 yds

DOLPHIN'S BARN

p130 p131 p132 p133
p134 p135 p136 p137

D

E

Victoria Quay

Rory O'More Br.

River

Mellowes Bridge

N4

St Paul's

Hammond Lane

Church St

Four Courts

Usher's Island

Arran Quay

Guinness Brewery
(St James's
Gate Brewery)

Island Street

Usher's Quay

Inns Quay

Father Mathew Bridge

Liffey

Bonham Street

Usher

Street

St Augustine

Merchants Quay

Watling Street

Bridgefoot

Oliver Bond Street

Brazen Head Pub

Cook St

St Audoen's

St Patrick's Tower

Bridge Street

John Street West

High Street

National College of Art and Design

Thomas Street West

Dept. of Social Welfare

St Augustine and St John

Cornmarket

Mother Redcap's Market

✠ **St James's**

Crane St

Thomas Crescent

St Catherine's

Vicar Street

Francis Street

J. Dillon Street

Tivoli Theatre

Iveagh Market

Portland St West

Rainsford St

Hanbury Lane

3

Guinness Storehouse

Robert Street

Bellevue

Earl Street South

Meath Street

Catherine St

Swift's Alley

Carman's Hall

St Nicholas of Myra

Francis Street

Bond Street

Meath Place

Liberty Market

THE

Newport Street

Pimlico

Ash St

Pim Street

Marrowbone Lane

Braithwaite St

LIBERTIES

The Coombe

Forbes Lane

Summer Street South

John Street South

Ardee Street

Weavers Street

2

Newmarket

Ward's Hill

New Bow South

Cork Street

Chamber Street

Mill Street

Brickfield Lane

Fumbally Lane

R110

Donore Avenue

Brown Street South

Ossory Square

Clarence Mangan

Malpas Street

Cameron St

St Thomas Road

Blackpitts

1

Donore Avenue

Susan Terrace

Donore Road

O'Curry Road

⊕ **Coombe Hospital**

St Teresa's

O'Donovan Road

Road

D

E

135

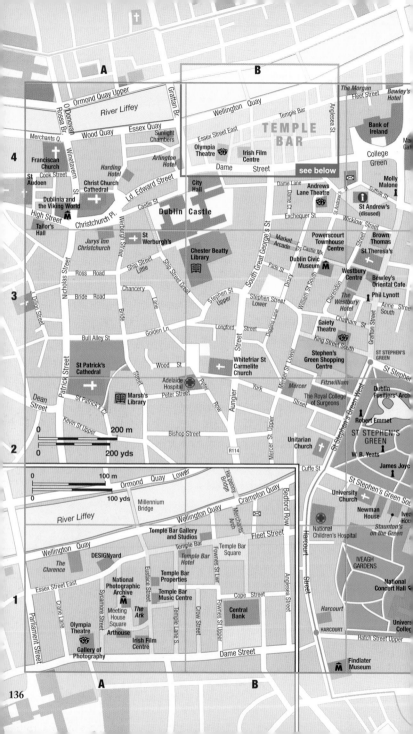

A

B

River Liffey

Ormond Quay Upper

O Donovan Rossa Br.

Grattan Br.

Wellington Quay

Temple Bar

The Morgan

Fleet Street

Bewley's Hotel

Merchants Q.

Wood Quay

Essex Quay

Sunlight Chambers

Essex Street East

TEMPLE BAR

Anglesea St.

Bank of Ireland

4

Franciscan Church

Winetavern

Harding Hotel

Arlington Hotel

Olympia Theatre

Irish Film Centre

College Green

St Audoen

Cook Street

Christ Church Cathedral

Ld. Edward Street

City Hall

Dame

Street

see below

Mary's Gate

High Street

Dublinia and the Viking World

Castle St.

Dublin Castle

Dame Lane

Dame Ct

Andrews Lane Theatre

St Andrew's

Suffolk St.

Molly Malone

Christchurch Pl.

Werburgh Street

Exchequer St.

St Andrew's (disused)

Wicklow St.

Tailor's Hall

St Werburgh's

Ship Street Little

Chester Beatty Library

Market Arcade

Castle Mkt

Powerscourt Townhouse Centre

Dublin Civic Museum

Brown Thomas

St Theresa's

Westbury Centre

3

Jurys Inn Christchurch

Ross Road

Chancery

Ship Street Great

Stephen St Upper

Fade St

Stephen Street Lower

William St. South

Drury

Clarendon St

The Westbury Hotel

Bewley's Oriental Cafe

Phil Lynott

Nicholas Street

Bride Road

Bride

Lane

Golden Ln.

Longford

Street

Diggs Lane

Mercer St. Lower

Gaiety Theatre

Chatham St

Anne Street South

Grafton Street

Dillon Street

Bull Alley St

Wood St

Whitefriar St Carmelite Church

King Street South

Stephen's Green Shopping Centre

ST STEPHEN'S GREEN

St Patrick's Cathedral

St Patrick's Cl.

Adelaide Hospital

Peter Street

Peter Row

Aungier

York

Mercer

Fitzwilliam

The Royal College of Surgeons

Dublin Fusiliers' Arch

St Stephen

Dean Street

Kevin St Upper

Marsh's Library

Street

Street

Mercer St. Upper

Robert Emmet

2

0   200 m

0   200 yds

Bishop Street

R114

Unitarian Church

St Stephen's Green West

ST STEPHEN'S GREEN

W. B. Yeats

James Joyce

0   100 m

0   100 yds

Ormond Quay Lower

Ha'penny Bridge

Crampton Quay

Cuffe St

St Stephen's Green Sou

River Liffey

Millennium Bridge

Wellington Quay

Merchants Arch

Bedford Row

Fleet Street

University Church

Newman House

Ivea Hou

Wellington Quay

Temple Bar Gallery and Studios

Temple Bar

Temple Bar Square

Harcourt Street

National Children's Hospital

Staunton's on the Green

The Clarence

DESIGNyard

Temple Bar Hotel

Fownes St Lwr

IVEAGH GARDENS

Essex Street East

National Photographic Archive

Eustace Street

Temple Bar Properties

Temple Bar Music Centre

Cope Street

Anglesea Street

National Concert Hall

1

Parliament Street

Crane Lane

Olympia Theatre

Sycamore Lane

Meeting House Square

The Ark

Arthouse

Irish Film Centre

Temple Lane S

Crow Street

Fownes St Upper

Central Bank

Harcourt

HARCOURT

Univers College

Gallery of Photography

Dame

Street

Hatch Street Upper

Findlater Museum

A

B

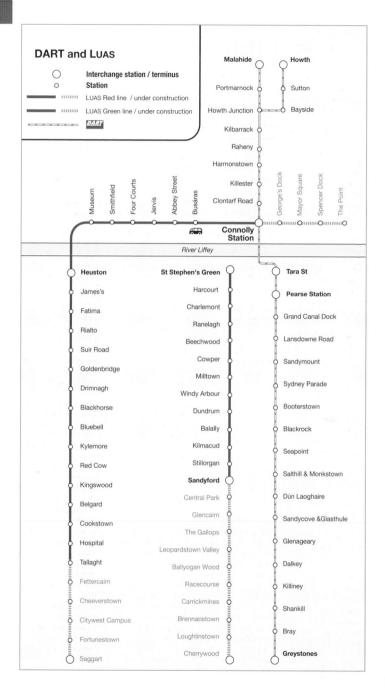

DART and LUAS

- ○ **Interchange station / terminus**
- ○ **Station**
- LUAS Red line / under construction
- LUAS Green line / under construction
- **DART**

Malahide   **Howth**

Portmarnock   Sutton

Howth Junction   Bayside

Kilbarrack

Raheny

Harmonstown

Killester

Clontarf Road

George's Dock   Mayor Square   Spencer Dock   The Point

Museum   Smithfield   Four Courts   Jervis   Abbey Street   Busáras

Connolly Station

River Liffey

Heuston	**St Stephen's Green**	**Tara St**
James's	Harcourt	**Pearse Station**
Fatima	Charlemont	Grand Canal Dock
Rialto	Ranelagh	Lansdowne Road
Suir Road	Beechwood	Sandymount
Goldenbridge	Cowper	Sydney Parade
Drimnagh	Milltown	Booterstown
Blackhorse	Windy Arbour	Blackrock
Bluebell	Dundrum	Seapoint
Kylemore	Balally	Salthill & Monkstown
Red Cow	Kilmacud	Dún Laoghaire
Kingswood	Stillorgan	Sandycove & Glasthule
Belgard	**Sandyford**	Glenageary
Cookstown	Central Park	Dalkey
Hospital	Glencairn	Killiney
Tallaght	The Gallops	Shankill
Fettercaim	Leopardstown Valley	Bray
Cheeverstown	Ballyogan Wood	**Greystones**
Citywest Campus	Racecourse	
Fortunestown	Carrickmines	
Saggart	Brennanstown	
	Loughlinstown	
	Cherrywood	

138

Atlas Index

PLACES OF INTEREST

139

Index

Insight Smart Guide: Dublin

Compiled by: Jackie Staddon and
Hilary Weston

Edited by: Sarah Sweeney

Proofread and indexed by: Neil Titman

Photography by: Alamy 34, 35B;
APA Glyn Genin 2B/T, 3BL/M, 7B, 9T,
10, 11B, 12, 13T, 15B, 18T, 19,
28/29, 30, 35T, 42-43, 42B, 43B,/M,
44/5, 45B, 46/47, 46B, 47, 48, 50,
52, 58B, 78, 79, 80BL/R, 83, 90/91,
108, 115R, 120T, 122B, 124/125,
127, 128; APA Corrie Wingate
3BR/MM/T, 4B, 11T, 14, 20, 21B/T,
25B/T, 28B, 29B, 36/37, 40/41, 40B,
44B, 48/49, 54, 55, 58/59, 60, 61,
74/75, 74B, 77, 81, 84, 85, 92,
97L/R, 100, 101, 107/B, 110,
111B,/T, 114/115, 114B, 116/117,
117B, 122/123, 123B, 126/127,
126B; Art Archive 65B; Axiom 33,
39B, 109, 118/119, 118B, 119B,
120B; Ibn battuta 16; The Clarence
67, 100/101; Corbis 36B; Dublinia
9B; Dublin Tourism 50/51, 54/55;
Everynight Images 63, 93, 94/95,
94B, 95; Fotolia 60T; Getty 91,
112/113, 113B; Mick hatford 99;
The Douglas Hyde Gallery 82/83, 82T;

Informatique 98B; Il Primo 103T;
John Jordan 112; Leeson Close 68B;
Leonardo 69, 71, 72TL; The Merrion
68M/T, 72/73; Original Print Gallery
88/89, 88B; National Photograhic
Archive 85; PA Photos 62/63 62B;
Istockphoto 38/39, 38B, 51, 53, 59B,
75; Rex Features 125; Kaihsu Tai
17T; Temple bar Gallery 84; Topfoto
64, 65, 76/77, 76B; Touchstone
Pictures 56/57; Ulster Bank Theatre
Festival 116

Picture Manager: Steven Lawrence
Maps: James Macdonald
Series Editor: Jason Mitchell

First Edition 2010
© 2010 Apa Publications GmbH & Co.
Verlag KG Singapore Branch, Singapore.
Printed in Canada

Worldwide distribution enquiries:
Apa Publications GmbH & Co. Verlag KG
(Singapore Branch) 38 Joo Koon Road,
Singapore 628990; tel: (65) 6865 1600;
e-mail: apasin@singnet.com.sg

Distributed in the UK and Ireland by:
GeoCenter International Ltd

Meridian House, Churchill Way West,
Basingstoke, Hampshire RG21 6YR;
tel: (44 1256) 817 987;
e-mail: sales@geocenter.co.uk

Distributed in the United States by:
Langenscheidt Publishers, Inc.
36–36 33rd Street 4th Floor, Long Island
City, New York 11106; tel: (1 718) 784
0055; e-mail: orders@langenscheidt.com

Contacting the Editors
We would appreciate it if readers would alert
us to outdated information by writing to:
Apa Publications, PO Box 7910, London
SE1 1WE, UK; fax: (44 20) 7403 0290;
e-mail: insight@apaguide.co.uk

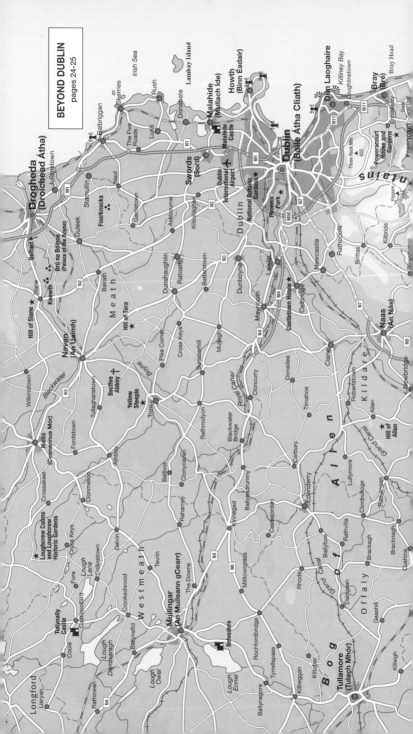